OAKVILLE
GROCERY

PROVISIONS

TO THE

GENERAL PUBLIC

OF

CALIFORNIA

SINCE 1881

THE COOKBOOK

SEASONAL RECIPES FROM
THE HEART OF
WINE COUNTRY

weldon**owen**

CONTENTS

Introduction 6 • A Brief History of the Oakville Grocery 9 • About This Book 11

SPRING

Family-Style Breakfast 19

Spa Lunch 30

Wine Country Picnic 38

Alfresco Garden Party 49

SUMMER

Sunday Sunshine Breakfast 64

Pool Party 75

Summer Family BBQ 85

California Coastal Picnic 99

FALL

Weekend Brunch with Friends 112

Autumn Harvest Picnic 123

Wine Country Cocktail Party 129

Fall Pizza Party 145

WINTER

Holiday Brunch Gathering 158

Afternoon Spritz Party 167

Winter Wine and Cheese Party 179

Wine Country Family Dinner 195

Pantry Staples 205 • Index 218

Introduction

The first time I set foot in the Oakville Grocery, I was just eleven years old and traveling from my native France through California with my sister and our grandparents. It was marvelous, and I still remember the awe I felt walking into this historic, rustic building. Now many years later and living in the Napa Valley, I still get that feeling every time I walk in.

In 2019, I had the opportunity to take over this extraordinary store, which is filled with the history of the area. Our vision is to celebrate the beauty and lifestyle of the Napa Valley by offering a carefully curated collection of locally grown and produced foods and wines to our customers. The Napa Valley is so much about the finer things in life. By making use of the incredible bounty available in this part of the world and bringing in the wonderful community of this valley, we aim to carry on the legacy of the Oakville Grocery and help herald it into a new era.

This book is a celebration. Of our customers, our employees, and the purveyors we work with. Of the beauty and lifestyle of the great Napa Valley. Of the history and relevance of the Oakville Grocery. Of the delicious food and drink we make and share with the community around us—a community we continue to build. The recipes in this book are an invitation to gather together with food and wine. I hope they spark an abundance of love and happy memories—and of more to come!

With passion,

Jean Charles Boinet

PHOTOGRAPH (ABOVE): LOWELL DOWNEY, ART & CLARITY
PHOTOGRAPH (OPPOSITE): ERIC WOLFINGER

A Brief History of the Oakville Grocery

The Oakville Grocery was already open in 1874, making it one of California's oldest retail businesses still in operation. It was originally operated by Patrick O'Neil, and its idyllic location in the heart of the Napa Valley anchored it to the landscape and surrounding community. Around this same time, as wheat began to decline in importance as a local cash crop and was starting to be replaced by vineyards, more and more wineries were springing up in the area.

Over the next few years, the store—called the Oakville Mercantile at the time—and the land it stood on changed hands several times. In 1877, the business was taken over by Jim McQuaid and his wife, Jennie, who eventually purchased the stately Victorian house next door and the acre of land it sat on. Jim not only ran the store but also served as the local railroad agent and the postmaster at the Oakville post office, which was housed in the building. Because of this, the store became a community hub and one of the few places that sold provisions in the area.

After Jim's death in 1889, Jennie married Melchior Kemper Sr., a flour miller based in Vallejo. They moved into the Victorian next door and continued to run the store. In 1893, a disastrous fire broke out, burning down the store, a blacksmith shop, a butcher shop, and a barn—essentially the entire commercial center of Oakville was destroyed in one night. The store was rebuilt, and in 1904, Jennie and Melchior Sr. sold it and the adjacent Victorian house to Joseph and Willis Booth—brothers and grocers—and their stepfather, Frederick Durrant.

The Booth brothers and Durrant reenvisioned the mercantile store as a grocery, and as the tiny town of Oakville grew, so did their customer base. They enlarged the store, and it quickly became the place that locals shopped for all of their necessities, from flour, eggs, and wines to clothing and chicken feed. It carried on in this fashion until 1920, when Prohibition forced vintners and saloonkeepers to close down their businesses. But instead of shutting down the store, sales started to boom as tourists from the Bay Area flocked to the Napa Valley for bootlegged wine and liquor. And while the Oakville Mercantile didn't sell wine at this time, it was well positioned to supply all other sundries and groceries to the out-of-town visitors, including sandwiches, ice cream, farm-grown produce, and other local amenities.

The Great Depression of 1933 followed on the heels of World War I and Prohibition. These three events nearly destroyed the Napa Valley wine industry, with many vineyards replanted with walnut and plum orchards. But the store kept chugging along, even while the wine industry hibernated. When World War II broke out in 1941, Napa suddenly experienced an influx of people working on the war effort, and the store saw an uptick in business.

Just before his death in 1943, Frederick Durrant sold the store, which then changed hands a couple of times before being purchased by Everett (Mike) and Elsie Giugni. The Giugnis updated the store and, over the next thirty years, ran it with their children, at times just scraping by while big new wineries were being constructed. By 1973, and after years of challenges, the store was seriously run-down. The Giugnis' daughter, Elsie Jane, and her husband, Wayne Malcolm, who had been running the store, were ready to sell.

The early 1970s heralded a new era of gourmet cooking, but contemporary or high-end ingredients and foods like pesto, crème fraîche, and pâté were virtually unobtainable in the Napa Valley. The timing was perfect. John and Pam Michels, the new owners, reimagined the store as an epicurean market filled with fine foods and upscale items. The redefined store reopened as the Oakville Grocery.

John and Pam decided to test the market demand for gourmet products in Oakville by offering more than six dozen types of prepared mustard. As soon as customers began buying up the mustards, artisanal cheeses, fresh herbs and exotic spices, an assortment of caviars, and other culinary items formerly unavailable in rural Napa Valley were added to the shelves.

The Michelses were careful to preserve the history and feel of the store while modernizing its physical features—coffee bar!—and inventory. Business was now booming in both the Napa Valley and at the Oakville Grocery, and the Michelses were overworked. In the late 1970s, they sold to

Joseph Phelps, a prominent vintner, with John staying on to manage the store. After opening a second store in San Francisco—to much acclaim but failing after only a year—Joseph and John parted ways.

The 1980s brought wealth, hundreds of new wineries, upscale restaurants, and another influx of residents to the Napa Valley. Joseph and his manager, Steve Carlin, enhanced the wine program in the store, emphasizing the relationship between good food and good wine and playing into the burgeoning culture and economics of the Napa Valley. And the Oakville Grocery was once again at the epicenter, considered "the best of the best." In the 1990s, the wealth in the Napa Valley grew steadily, and the store's combination of knowledgeable staff and luxury wine and fine foods continued to draw customers. The time was right to open other stores.

Over the next few years, Joseph and Steve opened four new stores: Palo Alto, Walnut Creek, Los Gatos, and Healdsburg. These branches, while customized to their locations, offered the high-end deli fare, culinary specialties, and prepared meals that customers had come to expect at the original location: grilled shrimp, pad Thai, arancini, house-made soups and salads made with hard-to-find ingredients, and dinners of crispy duck and leg of lamb. Shelves remained lined with a stunning array of local and imported cheeses, charcuterie, and obscure condiments. The newer stores even had a pizza oven, rotisserie, and wine tasting bar. Alongside these openings, the flagship store in Oakville continued to thrive.

In the early 2000s, things started to take a turn. The Walnut Creek and Los Gatos outposts closed, Joseph Phelps released his control of the store to an investment group, and Steve Carlin moved on to develop the San Francisco Ferry Building Marketplace and the Oxbow Public Market in Napa. The investment group had plans for a big expansion, but the economics of 2007 had put them into a financial quandary. It was at this time that entrepreneur and fine foods enthusiast Leslie Rudd stepped in and took over ownership of the store. Leslie closed the Palo Alto store and refined the selections in Oakville and Healdsburg.

By 2011, the original Oakville Grocery was in desperate need of renovation. The building was sagging, had never had a solid foundation, and needed insulation and plumbing and electrical upgrades. Leslie had a love of history and had restored a number of historical structures over the years, so with an eye to keeping the building's intrinsic beauty and original character intact, he salvaged all that he could while restoring both the store and the Victorian house next door.

In 2018, Leslie Rudd passed away, and the store was once again up for sale. Jean-Charles Boisset, who grew up in the Burgundy region of France and hails from a family of vintners who own historically significant wineries, saw a unique opportunity to own and nurture a piece of Napa Valley history. Jean-Charles's passion for history, authenticity, and synchronicity with the environment made the Oakville Grocery a perfect fit.

Jean-Charles has since guided the store in a new direction, one of artfully displayed and carefully curated local ingredients along with distinctive sandwiches, prepared salads, wood-fired pizzas, and more. Instead of the obscure, difficult-to-source ingredients of the past, the store is now focused on foods that are high-quality, sustainable, and almost always local. Alongside the store sits the original two-story Victorian home—now renovated and renamed the Durrant & Booth House and transformed into an interactive museum—and an expansive outdoor dining area with a wood-fired oven.

Through its nearly century and a half of history, the Oakville Grocery has always served as a welcoming meeting place for the area's residents and visitors. This iconic space survived an ever-changing economy, a catastrophic fire, the decline and growth of the Napa Valley, and the expansion of the local winemaking and culinary industry. The history of the area is reflected in the store, a hallmark of endurance and community. Always more than just a grocery store, it embodies the lifestyle of the region.

PHOTOGRAPH COURTESY OF LIN WEBER

About This Book

The Oakville Grocery draws locals and visitors alike for its friendly atmosphere, delicious food, and community spirit. Here you'll find breakfast fare with all-natural juices to fuel a busy day in wine country; locally produced artisanal foods perfect for a vineyard picnic; wood-fired pizzas for lunch on the outdoor patio; and colorful salads and sandwiches to take on the go—whether wine tasting, on a hike or bike ride in the nearby hills, or on a trip to the coast.

The more than one hundred recipes in this book are a celebration of all that the Oakville Grocery has to offer—meals that follow the seasons and are emblematic of the Napa Valley. Divided by season, each chapter is filled with our favorite suggested menus reflective of wine country living, whether it's a spa lunch with friends, a wine and cheese party, or a picnic among the vines. The recipes, like the Oakville Signature Salad with Grilled Chicken, Blue Cheese, and Marcona Almonds (page 123); Vegetable Romesco Sandwiches (page 105); French Country Pâté Snack Board (page 38); or Kale Salad Mezzaluna with Golden Balsamic Dressing (page 47), will take you on a trip through the Napa Valley and Northern California, evoking the local ingredients that go into everything we serve at the store.

We are excited to share this bounty—from our iconic sandwiches and the much-loved salads in our deli case to our famous mezzalunas, pizzas, and so much more. Let the recipes, stories, and photographs found in this book help guide you the next time you want to re-create a picturesque wine country picnic, an alfresco evening meal under twinkling lights, a festive weekend brunch, or a lazy afternoon spritz party. Until we meet again.

PHOTOGRAPH: ERIC WOLFINGER

MENUS

SPRING

Family-Style Breakfast

Spa Lunch

Wine Country Picnic

Alfresco Garden Party

RECIPES

FAMILY-STYLE BREAKFAST

Maple-Coconut Granola and Yogurt Parfaits 19
Rutherford Sandwiches 20
Yountville Sandwiches 22
Roasted Fingerling Potatoes with Peppers and Onions 23
Blueberry-Almond Streusel Muffins 26
Cold Brew Iced Vanilla Latte 27

SPA LUNCH

Hummus and Vegetable Crudités 30
Asparagus Soup with Lemon and Chives 31
Miyoko's Vegan Smoked Cheese Sandwiches 33
Spring Green Salad 34
Quinoa Salad with Tomatoes and Feta 36
Plant-Based Matcha Latte 37

WINE COUNTRY PICNIC

French Country Pâté Snack Board 38
Sesame Noodle Salad 39
California Cheese Plate with Stone Fruit Chutney 41
Francisco's Fried Chicken Tenders 44
Kale Salad Mezzaluna with Golden Balsamic Vinaigrette 47
Triple Chocolate Brownies 48

ALFRESCO GARDEN PARTY

Artichoke-Spinach Dip with Pita Chips 49
Vegetable Wraps with Roasted Pepper Hummus 50
Wagon Wheel and Rosemary Ham Sandwiches 51
Smoked Salmon Sandwiches with Skyhill Chèvre 53
Little Gem Salad with Herbed Green Goddess 54
Rocky's Reuben Sandwiches 56
Summer Fruit Rosé Sangria 57
Strawberry Cream Tartlets 59

FAMILY-STYLE BREAKFAST

Maple-Coconut Granola and Yogurt Parfaits

We make our granola with plenty of dried fruits, seeds, and nuts, loading it with flavor and nutrition. Making your own granola is surprisingly easy and leaves you room to customize it exactly how you like it. For a big family breakfast, put out bowls of the granola, yogurt, and fresh fruit and a pitcher of honey and invite guests to tailor their own parfaits.

MAKES ABOUT 10 CUPS GRANOLA

¼ cup dried currants or raisins

¼ cup dried cranberries

¼ cup chopped dried apricots

¼ cup chopped dried figs

3 cups old-fashioned rolled oats

1 cup coarsely chopped almonds

1 cup coarsely chopped walnuts

1 cup unsweetened dried coconut flakes

½ cup raw hulled sunflower seeds

2 tablespoons black or white sesame seeds, or a mixture

½ cup pure maple syrup, preferably grade B

⅓ cup honey

2 large egg whites, lightly beaten

¼ cup canola oil

2 tablespoons firmly packed light brown sugar

1 teaspoon ground cinnamon

½ teaspoon kosher salt

Position 2 racks evenly in the oven and preheat the oven to 325°F. Line 2 large sheet pans with parchment paper.

In a small bowl, stir together the currants, cranberries, apricots, and figs; set aside. In a large bowl, stir together the oats, almonds, walnuts, coconut, sunflower seeds, and sesame seeds. In another small bowl, whisk together the maple syrup, honey, egg whites, oil, sugar, cinnamon, and salt until the sugar dissolves. Pour over the oat mixture and mix well with your hands until evenly moistened. Divide the mixture between the prepared sheet pans and spread in an even layer.

Bake the granola, stirring every 10 minutes and being sure to move the granola from the edges of the pan into the center, until it is noticeably crispier, 45 minutes to 1 hour. Rotate the pans back to front and between the oven racks halfway through baking. As soon as the granola comes out of the oven, sprinkle it with the reserved dried fruit mixture, dividing it evenly between the pans, and stir to combine. Taste and adjust with more salt if you like. Let cool completely in the pans. Crumble into small clusters and clumps. (The granola can be stored in an airtight container at room temperature for up to 1 month.)

To assemble the parfaits, for each serving, layer the granola, yogurt, and fresh fruit in tall glasses or in bowls. Drizzle with honey and serve.

Note: For each serving, use ½ cup granola, ½ cup plain Greek yogurt, ½ cup diced nectarine or peeled and diced peach, or mango, and honey, for drizzling.

Oakville Grocery | The Cookbook

FAMILY-STYLE BREAKFAST

Rutherford Sandwiches

This bacon, egg, and cheese delight is the most popular breakfast sandwich on our menu. We use freshly baked ciabatta rolls from Berkeley-based Acme Bread, but you can use any artisanal roll you like. Be sure to purchase good-quality thick-cut bacon for the most delectable results.

MAKES 2 SANDWICHES

4 slices thick-cut bacon

2 ciabatta rolls, split

3 tablespoons unsalted butter, at room temperature

2 large slices Cheddar cheese

Mayonnaise, homemade (page 210) or store-bought, for spreading

2 large eggs

Kosher salt and freshly ground pepper

½ cup arugula (optional)

In a frying pan over medium-low heat, cook the bacon, turning once or twice, until the fat renders and the bacon becomes crispy, about 8 minutes. Transfer to paper towels to drain.

Brush the cut sides of the rolls with 2 tablespoons of the butter, dividing the butter evenly. Heat a large nonstick frying pan over medium heat and add the roll halves, cut side down, to the pan. Toast until golden brown. Transfer each roll, cut side up, to a cutting board. Wipe out the pan with paper towels.

Place a slice of Cheddar on the bottom half of each roll. Spread the top half of each roll with mayonnaise.

Return the nonstick pan to medium-low heat and add the remaining 1 tablespoon butter. When the butter melts and is foamy, crack the eggs into the pan and season with salt and pepper. Cook until the whites begin to set, about 2 minutes, then flip the eggs and cook for about 1 minute for over medium or 1½ minutes for over hard.

Place an egg on top of each slice of Cheddar. Top each egg with 2 bacon slices and then half of the arugula (if using). Season with salt and pepper. Cap with the roll top, cut in half, and serve.

FAMILY-STYLE BREAKFAST

Yountville Sandwiches

Many of the breakfast sandwiches found in our original Oakville store are named after the towns lining Highway 29 through picturesque Napa Valley. The tiny town of Yountville, which lies right in the middle of the valley, is a gem and is home to some exquisite restaurants. A stack of these hearty sandwiches at your next family gathering will appease even the pickiest morning eaters.

MAKES 2 SANDWICHES

2 ciabatta rolls, split

3 tablespoons unsalted butter, at room temperature

4 thin slices ham, preferably Fra' Mani

2 large slices Swiss cheese

2 large eggs

1 tablespoon milk

Kosher salt and freshly ground pepper

½ cup arugula (optional)

Brush the cut sides of the rolls with 2 tablespoons of the butter, dividing the butter evenly. Heat a large nonstick frying pan over medium heat and add the roll halves, cut side down, to the pan. Toast until golden brown. Transfer each roll, cut side up, to a cutting board. Wipe out the pan with paper towels.

Layer half of the ham and a slice of Swiss cheese on the bottom half of each roll. Set aside.

In a bowl, whisk together the eggs and milk, then season with salt and pepper. Return the nonstick pan to medium-low heat and add the remaining 1 tablespoon butter. When the butter melts and is foamy, add the eggs and cook until set into a thin, flat omelet, about 2 minutes. Remove from the heat and divide the omelet in half.

Fold an omelet half on top of each cheese slice. Top each omelet half with half of the arugula (if using). Season with salt and pepper. Cap with the roll tops, cut in half, and serve.

FAMILY-STYLE BREAKFAST

Roasted Fingerling Potatoes with Peppers and Onions

Small, short, and cylindrical, fingerling potatoes are perfect for roasting, turning out creamy on the inside and crisp and caramelized on the outside. Paired with sweet peppers and onions, they make an ideal side dish for a big breakfast or brunch—or for a satisfying family dinner alongside Herbed Roast Chicken (page 196).

MAKES 4 SERVINGS

1 lb fingerling potatoes, halved lengthwise

1 red bell pepper, quartered lengthwise, seeded, and cut crosswise into strips

1 small yellow onion, halved and cut into ¼-inch-thick slices

2 tablespoons olive oil

Kosher salt and freshly ground pepper

Preheat the oven to 425°F. Combine the potatoes, bell pepper, and onion in a large cast-iron frying pan or a sheet pan. Drizzle evenly with the oil and season with salt and pepper. Toss until evenly coated and spread in an even layer.

Roast, tossing occasionally, until the potatoes are tender and browned, about 30 minutes. Season with more salt and pepper if you like, then serve.

FAMILY-STYLE BREAKFAST

Blueberry-Almond Streusel Muffins

Blueberry muffins don't have to be boring—and ours are anything but! The baked goods we have at the store come from award-winning local bakers, but we couldn't resist giving you one of our favorite recipes to bake at home. This upgraded treat includes plenty of juicy berries plus an optional crunchy-sweet almond streusel topping.

MAKES 12 MUFFINS

Unsalted butter, at room temperature, for the pan

For the streusel (optional)

¼ cup all-purpose flour

¼ cup sliced almonds

2 tablespoons firmly packed light brown sugar

Pinch of kosher salt

3 tablespoons unsalted butter, melted

For the muffins

2 cups plus 1 tablespoon all-purpose flour

2 teaspoons baking powder

½ teaspoon kosher salt

½ cup unsalted butter, at room temperature

¾ cup firmly packed light brown sugar

2 large eggs

½ cup sour cream

1 teaspoon pure vanilla extract

1½ cups fresh or thawed frozen blueberries

Preheat the oven to 375°F. Butter 12 standard muffin cups or line with paper liners.

If making the streusel, in a small bowl, stir together the flour, almonds, sugar, and salt. Add the butter and mix with a fork until the streusel is evenly moist and crumbly. Set aside.

To make the muffins, in a bowl, whisk together the 2 cups flour, baking powder, and salt. Set aside.

In a bowl, using an electric mixer, beat together the butter and brown sugar on medium speed until lightened. Add the eggs one at a time, beating after each addition until fully incorporated. On low speed, add the sour cream and vanilla and beat until well mixed. Then add the flour mixture in two equal batches, beating just until combined after each addition.

In a small bowl, toss the blueberries with the remaining 1 tablespoon flour. Using a rubber spatula, gently fold the blueberries into the batter. Divide the batter evenly among the prepared muffin cups. If using the streusel, sprinkle on top of the batter, dividing it evenly.

Bake the muffins until lightly golden and set to the touch, 18–24 minutes. Let the muffins cool in the pan on a wire rack for 5 minutes, then turn them out onto the rack. Serve warm or at room temperature. Leftover muffins will keep in an airtight container at room temperature for up to 1 week.

FAMILY-STYLE BREAKFAST

Cold Brew Iced Vanilla Latte

Here is a recipe guaranteed to wake up your weekend breakfast crowd. Make the cold brew the day before the gathering, then about a half hour before folks are slated to arrive, whip up and steep the lightly sweetened vanilla milk. Once everyone is on hand, divide up the cold brew and milk and serve these iced lattes to your appreciative guests.

MAKES 4 SERVINGS

1 cup ground dark-roast coffee

4 cups water

1 cup whole milk or plant-based milk

¼ cup sugar, or to taste

1 vanilla bean, split lengthwise

Ice cubes, for serving

In a pitcher, stir together the ground coffee and water. Cover and let stand at room temperature for at least 12 hours.

In a saucepan over medium heat, combine the milk and sugar. Scrape the seeds from the vanilla bean pod and add the seeds and pods to the milk mixture. Bring the mixture just to a simmer and immediately remove from the heat. Let steep for about 20 minutes, then scoop out the vanilla bean pod.

Strain the coffee through a fine-mesh sieve into a second pitcher. Rinse out the first pitcher, then strain the coffee through a coffee filter into it. Fill 4 tumblers with ice cubes. Divide the coffee evenly among the glasses, filling them to within 1 inch of the rim. Top each glass with ¼ cup of the vanilla-flavored milk and serve.

LOCAL ARTISAN

OHM COFFEE ROASTERS

When he's not playing his electric guitar, founder Derek Bromley

is busy running Ohm Coffee Roasters, a hard-rocking coffee producer based in Napa. The name comes from "a measure of electrical resistance—something electrified and amplified." Following the musical theme, each of Ohm's four coffee blends—Full Stack, Half Stack, Tweed, and Handwired—are named after guitar amplifiers.

Derek's business evolved naturally. After working in New York as a sommelier and then starting his own wine-based business, he moved to California and into brand management in the wine industry. It was a Blue Bottle cappuccino that opened his eyes to the nuances of great coffee and its similarities to wine.

In an interview by Napa's Archer Hotel, Derek described his coffee philosophy by saying, "Two things are musts for Ohm: approachability—sharing good stuff with others, having fun—and keeping the focus on balance—where the bean came from, that you can taste it in the cup while also maintaining some of the natural sugars that tend to get lost in dark roasting. We want to keep the origin clear while bringing out the character of the beans."

The sought-after beans are found at upscale markets and eateries throughout the Napa Valley and are served as our house coffee at the coffee bars of both Oakville Grocery locations.

PHOTOGRAPHS: OHM COFFEE ROASTERS

SPA LUNCH

Hummus and Vegetable Crudités

Creamy, lemony hummus is a snap to make at home and a perfect partner to a spring platter of crunchy vegetables. You can serve the vegetables suggested here or use what you have on hand or what looks good at the market. Red and orange bell pepper strips, lightly blanched broccoli or cauliflower florets, or cherry tomatoes make great additions. Add some crunchy crostini (page 136), too, if you like.

MAKES 8 SERVINGS

For the hummus

1 can (15 oz) chickpeas, drained and rinsed

⅓ cup well-stirred tahini (sesame paste)

¼ cup fresh lemon juice

¼ cup water

1 clove garlic, chopped

2 tablespoons extra-virgin olive oil

½ teaspoon kosher salt

For the crudités

16 thin asparagus spears, tough ends removed

16 thin green beans, trimmed

12 baby or French radishes with some green leaves attached, halved lengthwise

4 small, thin carrots, peeled and quartered lengthwise

1 small English cucumber, sliced on the diagonal

To make the hummus, in a blender (preferably high-speed), combine the chickpeas, tahini, lemon juice, water, garlic, oil, and salt and blend on high speed until well mixed. Turn off the blender and scrape down the sides with a rubber spatula. Continue to blend until the mixture is very smooth, 1–2 minutes. If the mixture is very thick, blend in a little more water. Taste and adjust the seasoning with salt and lemon juice if needed. You should have about 2 cups. Transfer to a serving bowl and set the bowl on a large platter or board. (The hummus can be made up to 1 week in advance and refrigerated in an airtight container.)

To prepare the crudités, bring a large saucepan half full of salted water to a boil. Meanwhile, ready a large bowl of ice water. Add the asparagus and green beans and cook just until crisp-tender, about 1 minute. Drain and then plunge into the ice water to stop the cooking. Drain again and pat dry.

Arrange the asparagus, beans, radishes, carrots, and cucumber on the platter or board with the hummus and serve.

SPA LUNCH

Asparagus Soup with Lemon and Chives

Nothing screams springtime louder than grassy asparagus—a true harbinger of the season. We love asparagus in all its guises, but this velvety, citrusy soup is a particular favorite. Depending on the number of people and the rest of your menu, you can serve larger bowls as the centerpiece or kick off the meal with smaller portions.

MAKES 4–6 SERVINGS

1 tablespoon unsalted butter

2 tablespoons olive oil

2 small leeks, white and light green parts, finely chopped

1 russet potato, peeled and cut into 1-inch chunks

1 lb thick asparagus spears, tough ends removed, chopped into 2-inch pieces

4 cups chicken broth

Kosher salt and freshly ground pepper

Juice of ½ lemon

3 tablespoons crème fraîche or sour cream

1 tablespoon finely chopped fresh chives

In a large saucepan over medium heat, melt the butter with the oil. Add the leeks and sauté until softened, about 5 minutes. Add the potato and cook, stirring, until beginning to soften, about 5 minutes. Add the asparagus and cook until just tender, about 3 minutes. Pour in the broth and season with salt and pepper. Raise the heat to medium-high, bring to a boil, reduce the heat to low, cover partially, and cook until the vegetables are very tender, about 15 minutes. Remove from the heat, stir in the lemon juice, and let cool for a few minutes.

Working in batches, transfer the soup to a blender and purée on medium-high speed until very smooth. Return the soup to the pan over low heat and reheat, stirring often, until piping hot.

Ladle into bowls, garnish with the crème fraîche and chives, dividing them evenly, and serve.

SPA LUNCH

Miyoko's Vegan Smoked Cheese Sandwiches

Miyoko's Creamery changed the paradigm for plant-based cheeses with its wide array of plain and flavored cheeses and butters. In this incredible sandwich, its smoked vegan cashew mozzarella cheese takes center stage, layered with the lively flavors of our house-made olive tapenade, sweet caramelized onions, and balsamic glaze; a tangle of peppery arugula; and briny muffaletta mix.

MAKES 2 SANDWICHES

4 slices artisanal bread, such as Della Fattoria semolina bread, or 2 ciabatta rolls, split and toasted

4–6 oz Miyoko's Creamery's vegan cashew milk mozzarella, sliced

2 tablespoons vegan mayonnaise

¼ cup black olive tapenade, homemade (page 209) or store-bought

¼ cup store-bought muffaletta mix or olive salad (optional)

½ cup Balsamic Caramelized Onions (page 208)

⅔ cup arugula

1 tablespoon Balsamic Glaze (page 210) or aged balsamic

Kosher salt and freshly ground pepper

Lay the bread slices or roll halves (cut side up) on a cutting board. Divide the cheese evenly between 2 of the bread slices or between the roll bottoms. Spread the vegan mayonnaise and the tapenade over the cheese, then top with the muffaletta mix (if using) and the caramelized onions, dividing each ingredient evenly.

In a bowl, toss together the arugula and balsamic glaze and season with salt and pepper. Divide the arugula evenly between the sandwiches, piling it on top of the caramelized onions. Cap with the remaining 2 bread slices or roll tops, cut in half, and serve.

SPA LUNCH

Spring Green Salad

A springtime spa lunch wouldn't be complete without a gorgeous green salad loaded with all the young, tender vegetables of the season—think pea shoots, radishes, English peas, and asparagus. English peas are at their best early in the season, when they are tiny and sweet, but if you can't find them, substitute briefly blanched frozen petite peas.

MAKES 6 SERVINGS

2 cups fresh shelled English peas (about 2 lb unshelled)

2 lb thin asparagus spears, tough ends removed, chopped into 2-inch pieces

2 cups trimmed pea shoots

1 cup thinly sliced radishes

¼ cup chopped fresh basil leaves

½ cup Lemon Vinaigrette (page 213)

Kosher salt and freshly ground pepper

Bring a saucepan three-fourths full of salted water to a boil. Have ready a large bowl of ice water. Add the peas to the boiling water and blanch for 1 minute. Using a sieve, scoop out the peas and transfer them to the ice water until chilled. Then scoop the peas out of the ice water with the sieve and transfer to a large serving bowl.

Refresh the ice if necessary. Using the same boiling water, cook the asparagus until crisp-tender, about 1 minute. Drain the asparagus and transfer to the ice water. Drain again and transfer to the serving bowl with the peas.

Add the pea shoots, radishes, and basil and toss to mix. Drizzle with half of the vinaigrette and season with salt and pepper, then toss to coat evenly. Transfer to a platter or divide among individual plates and serve with the remaining vinaigrette alongside.

SPA LUNCH

Quinoa Salad with Tomatoes and Feta

Our Greek quinoa salad is a regular feature of the deli counter and an ideal vegetarian-friendly side dish for an alfresco gathering. This heart-healthy salad gets a burst of freshness from sweet cherry tomatoes and juicy cucumbers and pops of bright flavor from fresh herbs and briny olives and feta. Use white or red quinoa or opt for a blend.

MAKES 4–6 SERVINGS

1½ cups quinoa

3 cups water

Kosher salt and freshly ground pepper

1 cup Greek Feta Vinaigrette (page 214)

1 pint cherry tomatoes (10–12 oz), halved

½ large English cucumber, halved lengthwise, seeded, and thinly sliced on the diagonal

¼ red onion, thinly sliced

¼ cup pitted and roughly chopped Niçoise olives

¼ cup crumbled feta cheese

¼ cup coarsely chopped fresh flat-leaf parsley leaves

¼ cup coarsely chopped fresh mint leaves

Put the quinoa into a fine-mesh sieve, rinse thoroughly under running cold water, and drain.

In a saucepan over high heat, bring the water to a boil. Add the quinoa and ¼ teaspoon salt, stir once, and reduce the heat to low. Cover and cook, without stirring, until all the water has been absorbed and the grains are tender, about 15 minutes. Uncover, fluff with a fork, and transfer to a large bowl.

Add half of the dressing to the quinoa and stir to mix well. Add the tomatoes, cucumber, onion, olives, cheese, parsley, and mint, season with salt and pepper, and stir and toss to mix well. Taste and add more dressing if needed, then serve.

SPA LUNCH

Plant-Based Matcha Latte

Matcha, a finely ground green tea powder, gives this lightly sweetened plant-based drink a mellow vegetal flavor with just a hint of bitterness. Choose your favorite plant-based milk (we like coconut or oat milk), or use regular milk if you prefer. You can easily switch this warm latte to a cold refreshment by using cold milk and serving the drink over ice.

MAKES 4 LATTES

4 teaspoons matcha powder, sifted

1 cup very hot water

1 cup coconut milk or oat milk, warmed

Pure maple syrup, for sweetening (optional)

In a bowl, combine the matcha powder and hot water. Using a whisk, whisk the mixture vigorously until the mixture is foamy, about 1 minute. Whisk in the coconut milk. Divide the mixture evenly between 4 warmed mugs. Sweeten to taste with maple syrup (if using) and serve.

WINE COUNTRY PICNIC

French Country Pâté Snack Board

A breezy pâté board and a bottle of wine are the ideal way to kick off any wine country picnic or festive outdoor meal. This flavorful country-style pâté takes time to prepare, but the results are well worth it. Curing salt, which helps the pâté develop rich color, can be found in the seasonings aisle of well-stocked grocery stores, in butcher shops, and online. Purchase caul fat, which ensures the pâté retains its shape, from a butcher shop.

MAKES ONE 2-QUART PÂTÉ; 12–14 SERVINGS

¼ lb pork liver

2 cups whole milk

½ lb pork fatback, cut into ½-inch cubes

2 lb boneless pork shoulder, cut into 1-inch cubes

1 tablespoon coarse sea salt

¼ teaspoon pink curing salt #1

½ teaspoon freshly ground pepper

1 fresh or ½ dried bay leaf

2 allspice berries

2 juniper berries

¼ teaspoon each mustard seeds and sweet paprika

Pinch of freshly grated nutmeg

¼ cup each brandy and chicken broth

3 cups heavy cream

2 tablespoons fresh bread crumbs

1 piece caul fat, 16 inches square

Cornichons, grainy mustard, and baguette slices, for serving

The day before you plan to assemble and bake the pâté, put the liver and milk into a small bowl. In a large bowl, combine the fatback, pork shoulder, sea salt, curing salt, pepper, bay leaf, allspice and juniper berries, mustard seeds, paprika, nutmeg, and brandy. Using your hands, mix well. Cover and refrigerate both bowls overnight.

The next day, drain the liver, rinse well under cold running water, pat dry with paper towels, and cut into 1-inch cubes. Add to the pork mixture and mix well. Transfer the pork mixture to a food processor and pulse until finely chopped. Return the mixture to the large bowl.

In a medium bowl, stir together the broth, cream, and bread crumbs. Add to the meat mixture and mix with your hands. Return the mixture to the food processor and pulse until well mixed, 1 to 2 minutes; it will be a loose, wet mixture.

Preheat the oven to 300°F. Line a 2-quart terrine mold (or a 9 x 5-inch loaf pan) with the caul fat, allowing it to drape over the ends and sides. Tightly pack the meat mixture into the prepared mold and tap the mold on the work surface several times to eliminate any air pockets. Fold the overhanging caul fat over the top of the meat mixture to enclose completely. Cover the mold with its lid or aluminum foil and place it in a larger baking dish. Pour boiling water into the larger dish to reach halfway up the sides of the mold.

Bake the pâté, adding more boiling water during cooking if the level drops, until an instant-read thermometer inserted into the center registers 145°F, about 1½ hours. Remove from the oven. Remove the cover and top the hot pâté with a weight, such as a foil-wrapped brick, to press out any excess juices. Let cool to room temperature, then refrigerate, covered, for at least 2 days or up to 4 days before serving.

To serve, cut the pâté into ½-inch-thick slices. Place on a board and arrange the cornichons, mustard, and baguette slices around the pâté.

WINE COUNTRY PICNIC

Sesame Noodle Salad

Here is another fixture of our deli offerings, and its simplicity of preparation belies its depth of flavor. A tangy dressing of sesame and tahini bathes the noodles in a nutty richness that is offset by sweet carrots, bright green onions, and citrusy cilantro. The salad is perfect on a picnic alongside Francisco's Fried Chicken Tenders (page 44) or even on its own, straight from the deli counter.

MAKES 6 SERVINGS

1 lb fresh or dried Chinese egg noodles

2 tablespoons toasted sesame oil

1 cup Tamari-Sesame Dressing (page 214)

3 small carrots, peeled and shredded

3 green onions, white and green parts, thinly sliced on the diagonal

¼ cup chopped fresh cilantro, plus more for garnish

Toasted white sesame seeds, for garnish

Bring a large pot three-fourths full of salted water to a boil over high heat. Add the fresh noodles, stir to prevent them from sticking, and cook until just tender, about 3 minutes. (If using dried noodles, follow the timing on the package instructions.) Drain and rinse thoroughly under cold running water, then drain again.

Transfer the noodles to a large bowl, add the oil, and toss to coat. Cover and refrigerate until chilled, at least 1 hour or up to overnight.

Just before serving, drizzle the noodles with ½ cup of the dressing and toss to coat. Add the carrots, green onions, and cilantro to the noodles and toss to distribute evenly. If the noodles are sticking together, add more dressing as needed to loosen them, tossing well.

Garnish with more cilantro and the sesame seeds and serve, passing additional dressing alongside.

WINE COUNTRY PICNIC

California Cheese Plate with Stone Fruit Chutney

A variety of cheeses and accompaniments pairs perfectly with a pâté board, especially during a leisurely afternoon picnic among the vines. Among our favorite cheeses to include are Pennyroyal Farm's Velvet Sister and Laychee, Cowgirl Creamery's Mt Tam and Wagon Wheel, Point Reyes Original Blue, and Andante Dairy's Acapella, all produced locally. The chutney recipe yields a generous amount, leaving you plenty to enjoy on future cheese plates.

MAKES 4 HALF-PINT JARS CHUTNEY; 4-6 SERVINGS

For the chutney

½ cup golden balsamic vinegar

¾ cup sugar

1 lb peaches or nectarines, blanched and peeled

1¼ lb apricots, plums, or pluots, pitted and sliced

½ lb cherries, pitted and halved

1 teaspoon green cardamom pods

¾ teaspoon peppercorns, crushed

¼ teaspoon aniseeds

2 orange zest strips, each 1 inch wide and 2 inches long

1 cinnamon stick

For serving

1½ lb assorted cheeses, such as an aged cow or sheep's milk cheese, a triple crème, and a goat's milk cheese

Toasted walnuts, almonds, or hazelnuts

Crostini (page 136), or 1 baguette, cut into ¼-inch-thick slices on the diagonal

To make the chutney, in a large nonreactive saucepan, stir together the vinegar and sugar. Halve and pit the peaches and cut the halves into thick slices. Add to the pan along with the apricots and cherries. Stir the fruit to coat with the vinegar-sugar mixture. Put the cardamom pods, peppercorns, and aniseeds on a square of cheesecloth, tie the corners together with kitchen string, and add to the pan along with the orange zest and cinnamon stick. Let stand at room temperature for 1 hour.

Set the pan over medium-high heat and bring to a boil. Reduce the heat to medium-low and simmer, uncovered, stirring occasionally, until the mixture is thickened and almost jam-like, about 1¼ hours.

While the chutney is simmering, ready 4 hot, sterilized half-pint canning jars and their lids.

When the chutney is ready, discard the cloth bag, orange zest, and cinnamon stick. Ladle the hot chutney into the jars, leaving ¼ inch of headspace. Remove any air bubbles (slide a wooden chopstick or skewer along the inside edge of each jar) and then adjust the headspace if necessary. Wipe the rims clean and seal tightly with the lids.

Process the jars in a boiling-water bath for 15 minutes. Remove the jars from the bath, let cool completely, and check the seal. If the seal is good, the jars will keep in a cool, dark place for up to 1 year. If a seal has failed, store the jar in the refrigerator for up to 2 months.

To serve, mound some of the chutney in a serving bowl and place on a large platter. Arrange the cheeses, nuts, and crostini around the chutney and serve. Alternatively, layer a slice of cheese and a dollop of chutney on each crostino, arrange on a large platter, and serve.

LOCAL ARTISAN

POINT REYES FARMSTEAD CHEESE COMPANY

As a multigenerational, women-owned, and family-run business,

Point Reyes Farmstead Cheese Company makes its mission not only to produce incredibly great cheese in Marin and Sonoma counties but also to create a work environment that is both equitable and respectful. The company's high standards extend to keeping customers happy and prioritizing environmental sustainability.

The co-owners, all sisters, grew up on a dairy farm in Tomales Bay started by their parents in 1959. By 2000, the cow population had outgrown the size of the farm, so the sisters rethought the business and transitioned it into the popular artisanal cheese company it is today. They launched with their creamy Original Blue, a raw milk blue that is now synonymous with the brand—and still made on the farm in Point Reyes.

Their other cheeses, among them Toma, Gouda, and Quinta, are made at their facility in Petaluma using pasteurized milk from local California dairies that share the same farming philosophies.

Here at the Oakville Grocery we have a long history of selling local artisanal cheeses. This award-winning Tomales Bay company produces some of our favorite selections for sandwiches, cheese platters, or just for toting on a picnic with a baguette.

PHOTOGRAPHS: POINT REYES FARMSTEAD CHEESE CO.

WINE COUNTRY PICNIC

Francisco's Fried Chicken Tenders

Known for his cheerful, friendly demeanor, Francisco Vásquez López, a cook at our Oakville location, brings a smile to anyone he comes across. These mind-blowing fried chicken tenders are one of his superpowers. The secret is to brine the tenderloins in buttermilk, then dredge them in a well-spiced flour mixture before deep-frying them to a crunchy finish. If you're lucky, there will be a side of Francisco's house-made salsa (page 213) for dipping, though he's also partial to ranch dressing.

MAKES 4–6 SERVINGS

3 cups buttermilk

¼ cup plus 1 teaspoon kosher salt

2 tablespoons fresh lemon juice

1½ lb chicken breast tenderloins

2 cups all-purpose flour

1 tablespoon smoked paprika

2 teaspoons garlic powder

2 teaspoons onion powder

1 teaspoon freshly ground black pepper

½ teaspoon cayenne pepper, or to taste (optional)

Canola oil, for frying

Francisco's Tomato Salsa (page 213) or your favorite dipping sauce, for serving

In a large nonreactive bowl, whisk together the buttermilk, ¼ cup of the salt, and the lemon juice until well blended and the salt has dissolved. Add the chicken, stir to coat, cover, and let sit at room temperature for 30 minutes.

Drain the chicken into a large, fine-mesh sieve, discarding the buttermilk brine. Set aside.

In a wide, shallow bowl, whisk together the flour, paprika, garlic powder, onion powder, black pepper, cayenne (if using), and the remaining 1 teaspoon salt.

Pour the oil to a depth of 1 inch into a large, wide sauté pan or deep frying pan (no more than half full) and heat over medium-high heat to 350°F on a deep-frying thermometer. Set a wire rack over a sheet pan and set the pan near the stove top.

When the oil is hot, working in batches to avoid crowding, dredge the chicken tenderloins in the flour mixture, shaking off any excess, and add to the hot oil. Cook, turning once or twice with tongs, until crispy, golden brown, and cooked through, about 5 minutes. Transfer to the rack to drain. Repeat to cook all the chicken tenders the same way. Serve right away, with salsa on the side.

WINE COUNTRY PICNIC

Kale Salad Mezzaluna with Golden Balsamic Vinaigrette

Is it a pizza, or is it a salad? This mash-up is everything you want it to be! A crunchy pizza crust encases tender kale-cabbage salad dressed with a honey-sweet balsamic dressing. To take it for a picnic, precook the pizza dough and pack up the salad and dressing separately, then assemble the mezzaluna just before serving.

MAKES 2 MEZZALUNAS

Two 8-oz balls pizza dough, homemade (page 205) or store-bought

Semolina or fine cornmeal, for dusting

Olive oil, for brushing

Kosher salt and freshly ground pepper

1 large bunch lacinato (dinosaur) kale

1 cup finely shredded red cabbage

¾ cup Golden Balsamic Vinaigrette (page 214)

½ English cucumber, halved lengthwise, seeded, and diced

2–3 tablespoons unsalted toasted sunflower seeds

1 avocado, halved, pitted, peeled, and diced

If using homemade dough, cover the dough balls and let come to room temperature for 4–6 hours; for store-bought dough, let the dough come to room temperature for 2–3 hours.

About 30 minutes before you are ready to bake the pizza crusts, position a rack in the upper third of the oven, about 6 inches from the heat source, and place a pizza stone on the rack. Preheat the oven to 550°F (or as high as your oven will go). Once the oven comes to temperature, let the stone continue to heat for 15 minutes longer.

When the oven and the stone are preheated, turn off the oven and turn on the broiler while you prep the dough. Working with 1 dough ball at a time, on a lightly floured work surface, pull the dough into a thin round crust about 8 inches in diameter. Dust a pizza peel with semolina and slide the dough onto the peel. (If you don't have a peel, use a rimless cookie sheet or an inverted sheet pan.) Brush the dough with oil and season with salt and pepper.

Turn off the broiler and return the oven temperature to 550°F. Carefully slide the crust onto the hot pizza stone and bake until golden brown, 6–8 minutes. Using the peel, remove from the oven and transfer to a cutting board. Repeat with the second dough ball.

To make the salad, strip the ribs from the kale, then stack the leaves and thinly slice crosswise. Transfer to a bowl and add the cabbage. Drizzle with ¼ cup of the dressing, then use your hands to massage the kale and cabbage slightly to soften them. Add the cucumber, sunflower seeds to taste, and avocado and toss gently to combine. Season with salt and pepper and add more dressing if you like.

Divide the salad between the pizza crusts. Fold one side of each crust over the salad, cut in half crosswise, and serve with the remaining dressing alongside.

Oakville Grocery | The Cookbook   47

WINE COUNTRY PICNIC

Triple Chocolate Brownies

No sun-kissed picnic is complete without a sweet. Brownies are a great option when dining alfresco as they can be made ahead and easily packaged for transport. This decadent recipe uses three types of chocolate chips—semisweet, milk, and white—plus unsweetened chocolate for the base. Feel free to use any assortment of chocolate chips you like.

MAKES 9 BROWNIES

½ cup unsalted butter, cut into 4 pieces, plus more at room temperature for the pan

4 oz unsweetened chocolate, finely chopped

1¼ cups sugar

¼ teaspoon kosher salt

3 large eggs, lightly beaten, at room temperature

1 teaspoon pure vanilla extract

¾ cup cake flour

½ cup semisweet chocolate chips

½ cup milk chocolate chips

½ cup white chocolate chips

⅔ cup chopped toasted walnuts (optional)

Preheat the oven to 325°F. Line an 8-inch square pan with parchment paper, allowing the paper to extend a couple of inches on two sides. Lightly butter the parchment.

In a saucepan over low heat, combine the butter and unsweetened chocolate and heat, stirring often, until melted. Stir in the sugar and salt until the mixture becomes glossy. Remove from the heat and beat in the eggs and vanilla. Sprinkle the flour over the mixture and stir just until blended. Let cool for 15 minutes. Stir in all the chocolate chips and the walnuts (if using).

Transfer the batter to the prepared pan and spread evenly. Bake until a toothpick inserted into the center comes out with a few crumbs attached, 25–30 minutes. Do not overbake. Let cool completely in the pan on a wire rack.

Use the parchment overhang to lift the brownie "cake" out of the pan, then transfer to a cutting board and peel away the parchment. Cut into 9 squares and serve.

ALFRESCO GARDEN PARTY

Artichoke-Spinach Dip with Pita Chips

Get your garden party started with this never-goes-out-of-style spinach-artichoke dip. You can make the crunchy pita chips and assemble the dip in advance, then, when guests arrive, just pop the dip into the oven, pop open a bottle of sparkling wine, and serve. Alternatively, serve the dip with crostini (page 136) or fresh baguette slices.

MAKES 6–8 SERVINGS

For the pita chips

2 pita breads, each about 7 inches in diameter

2 tablespoons extra-virgin olive oil

1 tablespoon Italian herb seasoning

For the dip

1 package (10 oz) frozen spinach, thawed

3 tablespoons olive oil

1 small yellow onion, finely chopped

2 cloves garlic, minced

1 can (14 oz) artichoke hearts, drained and coarsely chopped

1 package (8 oz) cream cheese, at room temperature

1/2 cup mayonnaise, homemade (page 210) or store-bought

1/2 cup sour cream

2 teaspoons Worcestershire sauce

1/2 teaspoon cayenne pepper

1 1/4 cups shredded mozzarella cheese

3/4 cup grated Parmesan cheese

Kosher salt and freshly ground black pepper

To make the pita chips, preheat the oven to 350°F. Line a sheet pan with aluminum foil. Split each pita bread into 2 thin rounds. In a small bowl, stir together the oil and Italian seasoning. Stack the rounds and cut the stack—as if cutting a cake—into 6 wedges (for a total of 24 wedges). Brush the wedges on one side with the herb mixture. Transfer the wedges, oiled side up, to the prepared pan.

Bake the wedges, turning them over once halfway through baking, until they are light golden brown and crisp, 10–15 minutes. Set aside.

To make the dip, keep the oven on at 350°F. Put the spinach into a fine-mesh sieve and press out any moisture. Transfer to a cutting board and finely chop. Set aside.

In a large, oven-safe frying pan (such as cast iron) over medium heat, warm the oil. Add the onion and cook, stirring occasionally, until softened, about 3 minutes. Add the garlic and cook, stirring, for 1 minute. Add the artichokes and cook, stirring, until the artichokes release their liquid, about 5 minutes. Remove from the heat.

In a bowl, whisk together the cream cheese, mayonnaise, sour cream, Worcestershire sauce, and cayenne until somewhat smooth. Stir in 1 cup of the mozzarella and 1/2 cup of the Parmesan. Season with salt and black pepper and stir to combine. Add the mixture to the frying pan and stir gently, combining well with the artichoke mixture. Top the dip evenly with the remaining cheese.

Bake the dip until bubbly and the top and edges are golden, about 30 minutes. To brown the top a little more, turn the oven on to broil and broil until the top is browned to your liking. Serve hot directly from the pan with the pita chips for dipping.

Oakville Grocery | The Cookbook

ALFRESCO GARDEN PARTY

Vegetable Wraps with Roasted Pepper Hummus

Packed with fresh vegetables, these wraps make a colorful and versatile addition to any garden party. You can set them out whole or halved for a substantial serving, or slice them crosswise into bite-size portions for finger food. They can be wrapped in parchment for easy transport, too, making them good candidates for a road trip through wine country, a picnic on the beach, or just lunch on the go.

MAKES 2 WRAPS

½ cup hummus, homemade (page 30) or store-bought

2 tablespoons chopped jarred roasted red pepper

2 large flour tortillas, each about 9 inches in diameter

½ small cucumber, peeled and thinly sliced

1 large tomato, thinly sliced

½ large avocado, halved, pitted, peeled, and thinly sliced

1 cup alfalfa sprouts

Kosher salt and freshly ground pepper

In a blender or mini food processor, combine the hummus and roasted pepper and blend until smooth and the pepper is puréed.

Lay the tortillas on a work surface. Spread half of the hummus over each tortilla.

Arrange half of the cucumber slices on top of the hummus on each tortilla. Press down gently. Arrange half of the tomato and avocado slices on top of the cucumber. Sprinkle half of the sprouts over the tomato and avocado slices. Season with salt and pepper.

Working with 1 tortilla, fold about 2 inches of the right and left edges over onto themselves and press gently. Beginning with the rounded side closest to you, roll up the layered tortilla, holding the folded edges down with your fingers as you roll. Repeat with the second tortilla.

Place the wraps, seam side down, on a cutting board. Using a sharp knife, cut the wraps in half on the diagonal and serve.

ALFRESCO GARDEN PARTY

Wagon Wheel and Rosemary Ham Sandwiches

This deceptively simple sandwich demands exceptional ingredients. Choose the best-quality ham, cheese, and bread you can find. We recommend Fra' Mani rosemary ham, Cowgirl Creamery's Wagon Wheel cheese (an aged cow's milk cheese similar to Fontina), and an Acme torpedo roll.

MAKES 2 SANDWICHES

2 torpedo or hoagie rolls, split

¼ cup Dijon mayonnaise

6 oz Fra' Mani rosemary ham or other good-quality ham, thinly sliced

¼ lb Cowgirl Creamery Wagon Wheel, Fontina d'Aosta, Gruyère, or other aged cow's milk cheese, sliced

Lay the roll halves, cut side up, on a cutting board. Spread with the mayonnaise, dividing it evenly. Top the bottom halves first with the ham and then with the cheese, dividing them evenly. Cap with the roll tops and press gently. Cut each sandwich in half and serve.

ALFRESCO GARDEN PARTY

Smoked Salmon Sandwiches with Skyhill Chèvre

Layers of salty smoked salmon, tangy fresh goat cheese, piquant preserved lemon, pickled onions, and spicy arugula come together in a flavor explosion. You can serve these sandwiches on their own or as part of a larger sandwich selection. For smaller servings, cut each sandwich into quarters and spear each quadrant with a cocktail pick.

MAKES 2 SANDWICHES

4 slices artisanal bread, such as Della Fattoria semolina bread

¼ cup Preserved Meyer Lemon Aioli (page 212)

¼ lb fresh goat cheese, preferably Skyhill chèvre

6 oz thinly sliced smoked salmon

¼ cup Pickled Onions (page 208)

½ cup arugula

1 tablespoon chopped fresh tarragon

Lay the bread slices on a cutting board. Spread one side of each slice with the aioli, dividing it evenly.

Top 2 bread slices with the goat cheese, dividing it evenly and spreading it in an even layer. Layer each of the cheese-topped bread slices with half each of the salmon, onions, arugula, and tarragon. Top with the remaining bread slices and press gently. Cut each sandwich in half and serve.

ALFRESCO GARDEN PARTY

Little Gem Salad with Herbed Green Goddess

Creamy, herbaceous green goddess dressing makes just about anything better in our book. Here we use it to coat our favorite lettuces, crunchy-sweet Little Gems, and plenty of paper-thin spicy radish slices. This is a great salad to serve alongside a tray of just-made sandwiches or an array of pizzas. The dressing can also double as a dip for crudités.

MAKES 4–6 SERVINGS

For the dressing

1 cup mayonnaise, homemade (page 210) or store-bought

½ cup sour cream

1 clove garlic, minced

4 anchovy fillets in olive oil, minced

½ cup loosely packed finely chopped fresh chives

⅓ cup loosely packed finely chopped fresh flat-leaf parsley

3 tablespoons finely chopped fresh tarragon

1 tablespoon fresh lemon juice

1 tablespoon white wine vinegar or champagne vinegar

½ teaspoon kosher salt

¼ teaspoon freshly ground pepper

4–6 heads Little Gem lettuce, or more if very small, halved lengthwise

8 radishes, red or white tipped, trimmed and thinly sliced crosswise

To make the dressing, in a blender, combine all the ingredients and blend on medium-high speed until well mixed.

Arrange the Little Gems on a serving platter or divide evenly among salad plates. Sprinkle with the radish slices, drizzle with some of the dressing, season with salt and pepper if desired, and serve. Pass the remaining dressing alongside.

ALFRESCO GARDEN PARTY

Rocky's Reuben Sandwiches

The Reuben is a time-honored East Coast deli sandwich, but that doesn't mean we don't crave it here in Northern California wine country. In fact, our prep cook, Raquel "Rocky" Navarro, loves the Reuben so much that she came up with this recipe and added it to our menu. Our version doesn't stray far from the classic: we spread Thousand Island dressing made in-house on our favorite sandwich bread from local bakery Della Fattoria and then layer thinly sliced pastrami, crunchy sauerkraut, and nutty Swiss cheese.

MAKES 2 SANDWICHES

For the Thousand Island dressing

½ cup mayonnaise, homemade (page 210) or store-bought

2 tablespoons ketchup

2 tablespoons finely chopped dill pickle

¼ teaspoon sweet paprika

Kosher salt

4 slices artisanal bread, such as Della Fattoria semolina bread

6 oz thinly sliced pastrami

½ cup well-drained sauerkraut

4 slices Swiss cheese

To make the dressing, in a bowl, stir together the mayonnaise, ketchup, pickle, and paprika, mixing well. Season with salt.

Lay the bread slices on a work surface. Spread the dressing on one side of each bread slice, dividing it evenly. Top 2 bread slices with the pastrami, then the sauerkraut, and finally the cheese, dividing each ingredient evenly. Top with the remaining bread slices and press gently.

To grill the sandwiches, preheat an electric panini press on medium-low according to the manufacturer's instructions. Place the sandwiches, one at a time, on the preheated press and cook according to the manufacturer's instructions until the sandwich is warmed through and the cheese is melted, 6–8 minutes. Alternatively, heat a stove-top grill pan or heavy frying pan over medium heat. Add a sandwich and cook, pressing down firmly with a heavy lid and turning once, until the cheese melts, about 3 minutes on each side.

Transfer the sandwiches to a cutting board, cut in half, and serve.

ALFRESCO GARDEN PARTY

Summer Fruit Rosé Sangria

When spring begins to give way to warmer summer evenings, we start making this refreshing wine cocktail to serve at all of our gatherings. A colorful array of fresh berries and stone fruits infuses French-style rosé with sweetness and gives this beautiful blushing cocktail a festive air.

MAKES 6–8 SERVINGS

1 bottle (750 ml) Provençal-style rosé or other dry rosé

1½ cups white cranberry juice

1 pint fresh raspberries

1 pint fresh blackberries, or 2 cups pitted and halved cherries

1 nectarine, pitted and thinly sliced

1 white or yellow peach, pitted and thinly sliced

Ice cubes, for serving

In a pitcher, combine the rosé, cranberry juice, raspberries, blackberries, nectarine, and peach. Stir well. Refrigerate until well chilled and the flavors have blended, about 2 hours.

When ready to serve, fill glasses with ice. Divide the sangria evenly among the glasses and serve.

ALFRESCO GARDEN PARTY

Strawberry Cream Tartlets

Fresh fruit and creamy custard tartlets will always have our hearts, and these gorgeous gems are the perfect way to end a springtime meal. Juicy strawberries are at peak sweetness during spring, so put them to use any way possible while there's a surplus in the market. If you are pressed for time, use store-bought mini tartlet shells.

MAKES SIX 4½-INCH TARTLETS

For the pastry cream

1 cup whole milk

3 large egg yolks

¼ cup sugar

1½ tablespoons cornstarch

1 teaspoon pure vanilla extract

2 tablespoons sour cream

3 tablespoons strawberry or raspberry jam

1 tablespoon berry liqueur (optional)

2 cups hulled and sliced strawberries or mixed berries

6 fully baked tartlet shells (page 207)

To make the pastry cream, in a heavy saucepan over medium heat, warm the milk until small bubbles appear around the edge of the pan. Meanwhile, in a bowl, whisk together the egg yolks, sugar, and cornstarch until blended.

Slowly add the hot milk into the egg mixture while whisking constantly. Return the mixture to the saucepan and whisk over low heat until the mixture thickens, about 2 minutes. Stir in the vanilla. Transfer to a small bowl, cover with plastic wrap, pressing it directly onto the surface to prevent a skin from forming, and refrigerate until well chilled, about 2 hours, before using.

When ready to serve, add the sour cream to the pastry cream and stir until smooth. In another bowl, whisk together the jam and liqueur (if using). Gently fold the berries into the jam mixture until evenly coated.

Divide the pastry cream among the tartlet shells, spreading it evenly. Arrange the berry mixture on top, dividing it evenly. Remove the tartlets from their pans and serve.

MENUS

SUMMER

Sunday Sunshine Breakfast

Pool Party

Summer Family BBQ

California Coastal Picnic

RECIPES

SUNDAY SUNSHINE BREAKFAST
Quinoa Breakfast Bowls with Potatoes, Spinach, and Pesto 64
Avocado Toast with Toasted Pepitas and Chili Crisp 67
Maple-Glazed Bacon 68
Summer Fruit Smoothie 69
Currant Cream Scones with Strawberry Jam 70
Balsamic Bloody Mary 74

POOL PARTY
Hazel's Shrimp Ceviche 75
Pesto Pasta Salad 77
Provençal Tuna Niçoise Sandwiches 78
Caprese Sandwiches with Balsamic Glaze 80
BLTA Sandwiches 81
Peach Bellini 84

SUMMER FAMILY BBQ
Deviled Eggs 85
Watermelon, Heirloom Tomato, Feta, and Mint Salad 87
Classic Oakville Burgers 88
BBQ Pulled Chicken Sandwiches with Slaw 90
Oakville Potato Salad 91
Grilled Corn, Tomato, and Roasted Pepper Salad with Cilantro 93
Cucumber-Lime Agua Fresca 94
Triple–Chocolate Chip Cookie Ice Cream Sandwiches 95

CALIFORNIA COASTAL PICNIC
Peach and Prosciutto Flatbread 99
Curry Chicken Salad with Avocado 100
Summer Panzanella Salad 103
Gazpacho 104
Vegetable Romesco Sandwiches 105
Turkey, Bacon, and Tomato Sandwiches 106
Summer Berry Streusel Bars 107

SUNDAY SUNSHINE BREAKFAST

Quinoa Breakfast Bowls with Potatoes, Spinach, and Pesto

Our Healdsburg breakfast menu features this popular dish that is both warming and nourishing. To go from simply breakfast to a memorable Sunday morning spread, set out sides of toast, scones, and/or bacon and whip up a fun drink or two.

MAKES 4 SERVINGS

For the dressing

¼ cup basil pesto, homemade (page 209) or store-bought

2 tablespoons fresh lemon juice

2 tablespoons extra-virgin olive oil

¼ teaspoon fine sea salt

⅔ cup quinoa

1⅓ cups water

Kosher salt and freshly ground pepper

2 green onions, white and green parts, thinly sliced

¾ lb small Yukon Gold potatoes, cut into ¾-inch pieces

2 tablespoons extra-virgin olive oil

½ lb baby spinach

4 large eggs

1 ripe but firm avocado, halved, pitted, peeled, and thinly sliced

1 cup halved cherry tomatoes

To make the dressing, in a small bowl, whisk together the pesto, lemon juice, oil, and fine salt. Thin with a little water to a pourable consistency. Set aside.

Put the quinoa into a fine-mesh sieve, rinse thoroughly under running cold water, and drain. In a saucepan over high heat, bring the water to a boil. Add the quinoa and ½ teaspoon kosher salt, stir once, and reduce the heat to low. Cover and cook, without stirring, until all the water has been absorbed and the grains are tender, about 15 minutes. Uncover, fluff with a fork, and transfer to a bowl. Add 2 tablespoons of the dressing and stir to mix well. Add half of the green onions and toss to mix. Cover to keep warm and set aside.

While the quinoa cooks, make the potatoes. Fill a large saucepan half full with salted water, add the potatoes, and bring to a boil over medium-high heat. Cook, stirring occasionally, until just crisp-tender, about 10 minutes. Drain well in a fine-mesh sieve.

Wipe out the saucepan used for the potatoes and place over medium heat. Add 1 tablespoon of the oil and the potatoes, season with kosher salt and pepper, and cook, stirring, until the potatoes are browned and tender, about 5 minutes. Add the spinach and cook, stirring and tossing, just until wilted. Add 2 tablespoons of the dressing and toss until evenly coated. Remove from the heat and cover to keep warm.

To make the eggs, in a nonstick frying pan over medium heat, warm the remaining 1 tablespoon oil. Crack the eggs into the pan and season with kosher salt and pepper. Cover the pan, reduce the heat to medium-low, and cook until the whites are set, about 2 minutes for over easy eggs (or flip the eggs and cook to the desired doneness).

Divide the quinoa among 4 shallow bowls. Spoon the potato mixture atop the quinoa, dividing it evenly, then add the avocado and tomatoes. Top each serving with an egg, then drizzle with some of the dressing. Garnish with the remaining green onions and serve.

SUNDAY SUNSHINE BREAKFAST

Avocado Toast with Toasted Pepitas and Chili Crisp

Avocado toast doesn't have to be boring. We like to jazz up ours with nutty toasted pumpkin seeds and plenty of chili crisp drizzled over the top. Be sure to choose ripe but still slightly firm avocados and a sturdy, dense artisanal bread. For a heartier dish, top each serving of toast with a fried or poached egg.

MAKES 2–4 SERVINGS

4 slices artisanal bread, such as Della Fattoria semolina bread

Salted butter, at room temperature

2 medium ripe avocados, halved, pitted, peeled, and thinly sliced

Kosher salt and freshly ground pepper

4 tablespoons chili crisp

4 tablespoons pepitas, toasted

Extra-virgin olive oil, for drizzling

Toast the bread in a toaster, a toaster oven, or under the broiler. Spread one side of each slice lightly with butter.

Fan out an avocado half on the buttered side of each toasted slice. Using a fork, gently smash the avocado into the toast. Season with salt and pepper. Drizzle 1 tablespoon of the chili crisp over each smashed avocado half and then sprinkle with 1 tablespoon of the pepitas. Drizzle with a little oil and serve.

SUNDAY SUNSHINE BREAKFAST

Maple-Glazed Bacon

A platter of crispy, salty-sweet bacon is a great addition to nearly any breakfast or brunch table. This simple technique will take your bacon to the next level, and no one has to know how easy it is. For an extra kick, sprinkle the bacon with coarsely ground black pepper or Sichuan pepper toward the end of baking.

MAKES 6 SERVINGS

1 lb thick-cut bacon slices

¼ cup maple syrup, warmed

Arrange the bacon slices in a single layer on a large, rimmed grill pan or a large sheet pan and bake for 15 minutes. Remove the pan from the oven and pour or spoon off the excess fat. Brush the bacon slices evenly with the maple syrup, return the pan to the oven, and continue baking until the bacon is crispy, about 5 minutes longer. Meanwhile, line a large sheet pan with paper towels.

When the bacon is ready, transfer the slices to the prepared sheet pan and let drain for about 5 minutes, then serve at once.

Note: The bacon we like to use for this recipe is a wine country original. Journeyman Meat Co. (page 190) has partnered with us to produce a custom bacon that is first cured with a brine made from our Oakville Grocery Cabernet and then spends time in a smoker fueled with French barrel wood used to age the wine.

SUNDAY SUNSHINE BREAKFAST

Summer Fruit Smoothie

Blending a mix of frozen ripe stone fruits is a great way to beat the heat of summer. We've used plum, nectarine, and cherry here, but experiment with the same amount of whatever ripe seasonal fruits you have on hand. For example, peaches or berries would be a terrific addition.

MAKES 4 SERVINGS

2 plums, pitted and coarsely chopped

2 nectarines, pitted and coarsely chopped

1 cup cherries, pitted

½ cup fresh orange juice

6 tablespoons fresh lemon juice

1 teaspoon pure vanilla extract

Honey, for sweetening (optional)

Spread the plum, nectarines, and cherries in a single layer on a small sheet pan and put into the freezer until frozen, at least 2 hours.

In a blender, combine the frozen fruits, orange and lemon juices, and vanilla and purée, slowly increasing the blender speed to high, until smooth, 1–2 minutes. Add honey to taste if desired and purée briefly to combine. If the smoothie seems too thick, thin with a little water to the desired consistency.

Divide evenly between 4 glasses and serve.

SUNDAY SUNSHINE BREAKFAST

Currant Cream Scones with Strawberry Jam

A basket of buttery British-style scones, a pot of homemade strawberry jam, and a steaming cup of tea is welcome any time of the day. Serve these currant-studded delights at a casual Sunday breakfast or as an afternoon treat after a day of wine tasting. You can leave out the currants if you prefer, and you can skip the jam in favor of clotted cream or lemon curd.

MAKES 8 SCONES

For the jam

1 lb strawberries, hulled and chopped

1 cup sugar

2 tablespoons fresh lemon juice

For the scones

2 cups all-purpose flour

¼ cup sugar

2½ teaspoons baking powder

½ teaspoon kosher salt

½ cup cold unsalted butter, cut into small pieces

½ cup dried currants

1 cup heavy cream

Unsalted butter, at room temperature, for serving

To make the jam, place 2 saucers in the freezer to chill. In a saucepan, combine the strawberries, sugar, and lemon juice. Bring to a boil over medium heat, stirring constantly to dissolve the sugar. Reduce the heat to medium-low and cook uncovered, stirring occasionally, until the berries are tender and the juices have thickened, about 10 minutes. To test, remove a chilled saucer from the freezer. Spoon about 1 teaspoon of the strawberry liquid onto the saucer and let stand for 15 seconds. If the liquid thickens to a jam-like consistency, the jam is ready. If not, cook for a minute or two longer and test again. Remove from the heat and set aside to cool. (The jam can be made up to 2 weeks in advance and refrigerated in an airtight container.)

Meanwhile, make the scones. Preheat the oven to 400°F. Line a sheet pan with parchment paper.

In a food processor, combine the flour, sugar, baking powder, and salt and pulse briefly to mix. Sprinkle the butter over the flour mixture and pulse until the mixture forms coarse crumbs about the size of small peas. Transfer to a bowl and stir in the currants. Pour the cream over the dry ingredients and stir with a fork or rubber spatula just until the dry ingredients are evenly moistened.

Turn the dough out onto a lightly floured work surface. Using floured hands, knead gently just until it clings together, then pat into a round about ½ inch thick. Using a 3-inch round biscuit cutter, cut out as many dough rounds as possible and transfer to the prepared pan, spacing them 1 inch apart. Gather up the dough scraps, pat them into a round, cut out more rounds, and add them to the pan. You should have 8 scones total.

Bake the scones until golden brown, 17–20 minutes. Transfer to a wire rack to cool. Serve warm or at room temperature, with the strawberry jam and butter on the side.

LOCAL ARTISAN

MODEL BAKERY

When most people think of the Model Bakery, a mainstay in Napa for over ninety years,

the first thing that comes to mind are its pillowy English muffins. Visitors making the trek from all over the country for a bag of these baked goods put Model on the map of national food destinations.

But the Model Bakery is more than just its famed muffins. Owned by Karen Mitchell and her daughter, Sarah Mitchell Hansen, it is also known for its comforting, familiar flavors that come through in buttery pastries, world-class breads, crisp cookies, and excellent breakfast and lunch fare.

In 1984, Karen, then a successful caterer, took over the business with a dream of using her family recipes and knowledge from travels throughout Europe to transform it into a European-style bakery. As she recalled in *The Model Bakery Cookbook*, published in 2013, her "goal was to provide the area with the kind of small-town bakery that was fast disappearing, a place where kids would stop by on the way home from school for a cookie, or where a customer could pick up a delicious birthday cake at a moment's notice."

Today, with three locations in the Napa Valley and a fourth location opening soon in Walnut Creek, the bakery has expanded into wholesale production but still supplies local businesses like the Oakville Grocery with its famous English muffins and other baked treats.

PHOTOGRAPHS: JOHN KLYCINSKI

SUNDAY SUNSHINE BREAKFAST

Balsamic Bloody Mary

A dash of balsamic vinegar adds just the right note of sweetness to these savory tomato cocktails. We've kept the embellishments simple, but if you favor a more festive array of garnishes, celery sticks, pickled green beans, or stuffed green olives would all be excellent.

MAKES 4 COCKTAILS

Ice cubes, for serving

8 oz JCB Pure Vodka or other vodka, chilled

16 oz tomato juice, chilled

¾ oz balsamic vinegar

1 tablespoon prepared horseradish

1 barspoon Worcestershire sauce

4 dashes of Tabasco sauce

¼ teaspoon celery salt

Juice of 2 limes

Freshly ground pepper

4 cherry tomatoes, for garnish

4 green chiles, for garnish

Fill 4 tall glasses with ice.

In a large pitcher, combine the vodka, tomato juice, vinegar, horseradish, Worcestershire sauce, Tabasco sauce, celery salt, and lime juice. Stir to mix well. Season with pepper.

Pour into the ice-filled glasses, dividing evenly. Garnish each glass with a cherry tomato and a chile speared on a toothpick and serve.

POOL PARTY

Hazel's Shrimp Ceviche

It's always a lucky day when we have fresh shrimp on hand and chef Hazel makes her amazing shrimp ceviche (we guarantee it doesn't last long around here). The shrimp are lightly poached, "pickled" in a mix of lime juice, jalapeños, and jalapeño juice, and then tossed with sweet mango, fresh cucumber, and crunchy jicama. If you like, add diced ripe but firm avocado and some chopped fresh cilantro with the mango.

MAKES 6 SERVINGS

For the poached shrimp

4 cups water

1 tablespoon Old Bay Seasoning

2 teaspoons kosher salt

½ teaspoon freshly ground pepper

1 bay leaf

2 lemon slices

1 lb small or medium shrimp in the shell, peeled and deveined

For the ceviche

½ cup fresh lime juice

¼ cup finely diced red onion

3 tablespoons finely diced pickled jalapeño chile

3 tablespoons jalapeño pickling liquid

Kosher salt and freshly ground pepper

½ cup diced fresh mango

½ cup peeled and diced English cucumber

½ cup peeled and diced jicama

Tortilla chips, for serving

To poach the shrimp, fill a bowl with ice water and set it near the stove. Pour the water into a saucepan, then stir in the Old Bay, salt, pepper, bay leaf, and lemon slices. Bring to a boil over medium-high heat. Remove the saucepan from the heat and add the shrimp. Set aside until the shrimp are bright pink and just cooked through but still tender, 3–5 minutes; do not overcook. Using a slotted spoon, transfer the shrimp to the ice water. Set aside until chilled, then transfer the shrimp to a cutting board and cut into bite-size pieces.

To make the ceviche, transfer the shrimp to a glass or ceramic bowl. Add the lime juice, onion, pickled jalapeño, and pickling liquid and stir well. Season with salt and pepper. Cover and refrigerate for 30 minutes.

Just before serving, stir in the mango, cucumber, and jicama. Taste and adjust the seasoning with salt and pepper if needed. Serve with tortilla chips for scooping.

POOL PARTY

Pesto Pasta Salad

This family-friendly pasta salad comes together in a snap and is great for a summer party, whether poolside or on a picnic blanket under the redwoods or at the beach. Look for the small balls of fresh mozzarella labeled ciliegine—"cherries"—or cut a large ball into small cubes. We love to use pasta from our friends at Bayview Pasta for this delicious dish.

MAKES 4–6 SERVINGS

Kosher salt and freshly ground black pepper

1 lb orecchiette or other short pasta

3 tablespoons extra-virgin olive oil

½ preserved Meyer lemon, homemade (page 207) or store-bought (optional)

1 lb cherry or grape tomatoes, halved or quartered

½ lb fresh mozzarella ciliegine (cherry size), halved

1 cup basil pesto, homemade (page 209) or store-bought, plus more as needed

¼ cup grated Parmesan cheese

2 tablespoons fresh lemon juice (optional)

Pinch of red pepper flakes (optional)

Bring a large pot three-fourths full of water (at least 4 quarts) to a rapid boil over high heat. Add 1 tablespoon salt and the pasta and stir for the first minute of cooking and occasionally thereafter. Cook until al dente, according to the package instructions. Drain into a colander and rinse under cold running water until cooled. Drain again, shaking out the excess moisture. Transfer to a large, wide serving bowl. Drizzle with the oil, toss to coat evenly, and set aside to cool completely.

If using the preserved lemon, remove and discard the pulp, then rinse and mince the peel. Add to the bowl with the pasta.

Add the tomatoes, mozzarella, pesto, Parmesan, lemon juice (if using), and pepper flakes (if using) and toss to coat evenly, adding more pesto if needed to loosen the pasta. Taste and adjust the seasoning with salt, black pepper, and lemon juice if needed, then serve. (The salad can be made up to 2 hours in advance and kept at room temperature; do not refrigerate.)

Oakville Grocery | The Cookbook

POOL PARTY

Provençal Tuna Niçoise Sandwiches

From the Provence region of France to Northern California wine country, salade Niçoise is much-loved summer fare, a welcome meal when temperatures start to rise. Transform the flavors and ingredients of this classic salad into sandwiches and you have easy-to-transport poolside or picnic fare.

MAKES 2 LARGE SANDWICHES

For the salad

2 cans (5 oz each) wild albacore tuna in water, drained

¼ cup mayonnaise, homemade (page 210) or store-bought

2 tablespoons finely chopped jarred piquillo or roasted red pepper

2 tablespoons chopped pitted Niçoise or Kalamata olives

4 slices artisanal bread, such as Della Fattoria semolina bread

¼ cup Caper Aioli (page 211)

¼ cup black olive tapenade, homemade (page 209) or store-bought

2 slices shaved red onion

2 jarred piquillo or roasted red peppers, cut into strips

2 hard-cooked eggs, peeled and thinly sliced lengthwise

1 cup arugula

Extra-virgin olive oil, for drizzling

Balsamic Glaze (page 210) or balsamic vinegar, for drizzling

Kosher salt and freshly ground pepper

To make the salad, flake the tuna into a bowl. Add the mayonnaise, piquillo pepper, and olives and stir to mix well.

Lay the bread slices on a cutting board. Spread one side of each slice with the aioli, dividing it evenly. Divide the tapenade evenly between 2 of the bread slices, spreading it evenly. Top each tapenade-covered bread slice with half of the tuna salad, spreading it into a thick, even layer. Top the tuna salad with the onion, then the piquillo pepper, and finally the eggs, dividing them evenly.

In a small bowl, drizzle the arugula with a little oil and balsamic glaze, toss to coat evenly, and then season with salt and pepper. Divide the arugula evenly between the sandwiches.

Top with the remaining bread slices and press gently. Cut each sandwich in half and serve.

POOL PARTY

Caprese Sandwiches with Balsamic Glaze

Crusty baguette stuffed with fresh mozzarella, ripe tomato slices, aromatic basil leaves—this simple sandwich is a summertime treat. Because it is made with only a few ingredients, choose just-baked bread from a local bakery, good-quality mozzarella, and peak-of-season tomatoes, preferably heirloom or beefsteak. And be sure to add the balsamic glaze—it's our secret touch!

MAKES 2 SANDWICHES

Two 8-inch lengths rustic baguette, split

4 tablespoons extra-virgin olive oil

4 tablespoons Balsamic Glaze (page 210)

8 slices fresh mozzarella cheese

8 tomato slices

12 fresh basil leaves

Kosher salt and freshly ground pepper

Lay the baguette halves, cut side up, on a cutting board. Drizzle each cut side with 1 tablespoon each of the oil and balsamic glaze. Layer the bottom baguette halves with the mozzarella, tomato, and basil, dividing them evenly. Season with salt and pepper. Cap the sandwiches with the baguette tops, cut in half, and serve.

POOL PARTY

BLTA Sandwiches

The time-honored BLT gets the California treatment with the addition of creamy avocado and garlicky aioli. Although it's best enjoyed in summer, when seasonal tomatoes fill local markets, you can make it in winter with slow-roasted tomatoes. For a big party, build mini versions on slider rolls.

MAKES 2 SANDWICHES

8 slices thick-cut bacon

4 slices artisanal bread, such as Della Fattoria semolina bread

¼ cup Garlic Aioli (page 211)

1 small avocado, halved, pitted, peeled, and sliced

6 tomato slices

2 large lettuce leaves

In a frying pan over medium-low heat, cook the bacon, turning once or twice, until the fat renders and the bacon becomes crispy, about 8 minutes. Transfer to paper towels to drain.

Lay the bread slices on a cutting board. Spread one side of each bread slice with the aioli, dividing it evenly. Arrange an avocado half on 2 of the aioli-covered slices, spreading the slices in an even layer. Using a fork, gently press the avocado into the bread.

Top each avocado-covered bread slice first with 4 bacon slices and then with 3 tomato slices, layering them evenly. Finish with a lettuce leaf. Top with the remaining bread slices, cut each sandwich in half, and serve.

Oakville Grocery | The Cookbook   81

POOL PARTY

Peach Bellini

Named for the fifteenth-century Venetian painter Giovanni Bellini, the true Bellini, which originated in Venice, Italy, in the 1930s, is made with white peach purée and sparkling wine. We've re-created this refreshing Italian cocktail because it is enjoyable anywhere. We recommend using peak-season peaches (or even nectarines) and a fruity sparkling wine—perhaps one from Napa Valley.

MAKES 4 COCKTAILS

1 ripe white or yellow peach, halved and pitted but not peeled, cut into 1-inch cubes

1 barspoon fresh lemon juice

1 barspoon Simple Syrup (page 215)

16 oz JCB Champagne or sparkling wine

Put 4 champagne flutes into the freezer at least 15 minutes before serving.

In a blender, combine the peach, lemon juice, and simple syrup and purée until smooth.

Divide the peach purée evenly among the chilled flutes. Top with the Champagne, stir gently to mix, and serve.

SUMMER FAMILY BBQ

Deviled Eggs

This is the classic version of this traditional appetizer, and we hope it never goes out of style. It's a recipe worth putting on repeat for any party, picnic, or other gathering. A day ahead of your get-together, cook the eggs, then cool, peel, halve, and remove the yolks. Make the yolk filling, refrigerate the whites and filling separately, and put the stuffed eggs together shortly before serving.

MAKES 24 STUFFED EGGS

12 large eggs

½ cup Dijon mayonnaise

½ teaspoon kosher salt

½ teaspoon smoked paprika, plus more for garnish

¼ teaspoon freshly ground pepper

Have ready a large bowl of ice water. Fill a large saucepan half full of water and bring to a boil over high heat. Using a slotted spoon, carefully add the eggs to the boiling water. Reduce the heat to medium so the water is at a gentle boil and cook the eggs for 11 minutes.

Using the slotted spoon, transfer the eggs to the ice water. Let sit for 10 minutes. Then gently crack each egg against a work surface, rolling it back and forth under your hand, to crack the shell finely all over. Peel off the shell. Cut each egg in half lengthwise.

Using a spoon, scoop the yolks out of the egg whites into a bowl. Place the egg-white halves, hollow side up, on a large serving platter. Add the mayonnaise, salt, paprika, and pepper to the yolks and, using a fork, mash them to a smooth, fluffy paste.

Spoon the yolk mixture into the egg-white halves, dividing it evenly and shaping it into a mound. Sprinkle each mound with a pinch of paprika and serve. The eggs can be made and refrigerated for up to 8 hours in advance before serving.

SUMMER FAMILY BBQ

Watermelon, Heirloom Tomato, Feta, and Mint Salad

Refreshingly crisp, cool, and sweet-salty, this salad tastes like summer in a bowl. It makes a terrific side dish to nearly anything barbecued or any of our sandwiches. Make sure to start with a cold watermelon, use the best tomatoes you can find, and seek out a good-quality cheese, such as a briny Greek sheep's milk feta or a mild and creamy French feta.

MAKES 6 SERVINGS

1 mini seedless watermelon, about 4 lb, chilled

1¾ lb assorted heirloom tomatoes and cherry tomatoes, halved, seeded, and sliced or cut into 1-inch pieces

2 Persian cucumbers, thinly sliced

2 tablespoons extra-virgin olive oil

2 tablespoons white balsamic vinegar

3 oz feta cheese, crumbled

½ cup fresh mint leaves, roughly chopped

Quarter the watermelon lengthwise and cut the flesh away from the rind. Cut the flesh into 1-inch cubes.

In a large, shallow serving bowl, gently toss together the watermelon, tomatoes, and cucumbers. Drizzle the oil and vinegar evenly over the mixture, then toss again to coat evenly. Sprinkle with the cheese and mint, and serve.

SUMMER FAMILY BBQ

Classic Oakville Burgers

For an easy summer barbecue, you can't beat a good burger. Purchase high-quality beef—local, organic, and/or grass-fed—with a bit of fat to it (80/20) to keep the burgers juicy. Our ultimate version includes caramelized onions, chili crisp mayo, and plenty of pickle and tomato slices. If you like, add slices of crisp-cooked applewood bacon or creamy avocado.

MAKES 4 BURGERS

1½ lb ground chuck

1 teaspoon kosher salt

½ teaspoon freshly ground pepper

Canola oil, for the grill grate

4 large slices Cheddar cheese

4 burger buns, split

½ cup Chili Crisp Mayonnaise (page 210)

½ cup Balsamic Caramelized Onions (page 208)

8 tomato slices

8 long dill pickle slices

¼ lb mixed salad greens

In a bowl, combine the ground chuck, salt, and pepper and, using your hands, mix together lightly just until the meat is evenly seasoned. Do not overmix. Divide into 4 equal portions and form each portion into a patty about ¾ inch thick.

Prepare a fire in a charcoal or gas grill for direct cooking over medium heat (350°F–400°F). Brush the grill grate clean, then oil the grate. Grill the patties, turning once, for about 6 minutes total for medium-rare or 10 minutes total for medium. During the last minute of cooking, top each patty with a cheese slice and cover the grill just until the cheese melts. Transfer the patties to a sheet pan. Grill the buns, cut side down, until toasted, 1–2 minutes.

To assemble the burgers, lay the bun halves, toasted side up, on a work surface and spread with the mayonnaise, dividing it evenly. Divide the caramelized onions evenly among the bun bottoms and top each with a patty. Layer each patty with 2 tomato slices followed by 2 pickle slices, then finish with one-fourth of the greens. Cap with the bun tops and serve.

SUMMER FAMILY BBQ

BBQ Pulled Chicken Sandwiches with Slaw

No one will ever know that you made this tender, smoky-sweet pulled chicken the day before in a slow cooker. It's a great way to extend the options for a big family barbecue without standing over the grill all day long (save that for the burgers!). The slaw is optional, but we love the tangy crunch it adds to this hearty sandwich.

MAKES 4–6 SANDWICHES

3 lb boneless, skinless chicken thighs

Kosher salt and freshly ground pepper

1 tablespoon olive oil

2¼ cups Chipotle Barbecue Sauce (page 212) or your favorite barbecue sauce

For the slaw

2 cups shredded napa cabbage

2 cups shredded red cabbage

¼ cup minced red onion

¼ cup mayonnaise, homemade (page 210) or store-bought

2 teaspoons country or regular Dijon mustard

2 teaspoons cider vinegar

1 teaspoon sugar

Kosher salt and freshly ground pepper

4–6 pretzel buns or burger buns, split

Season the chicken all over with salt and pepper. In a large frying pan over high heat, warm the oil. Working in batches, add the chicken and cook, turning once, until browned on both sides, about 3 minutes per side. Transfer to a slow cooker. Add the barbecue sauce and stir to coat evenly. Cover and cook on high until the chicken falls apart into shreds when prodded with a fork, about 2 hours. Alternatively, brown the chicken as directed, return all the chicken to the pan, add the sauce, stir to coat evenly, cover, and cook over low heat, stirring every now and again to prevent sticking, until very tender, about 1 hour.

Transfer the chicken to a cutting board. When it is cool enough to handle, shred with 2 forks.

Return the chicken to the sauce, stir to coat, and keep warm.

Meanwhile, make the slaw. In a large bowl, combine the cabbages and onion. In a small bowl, whisk together the mayonnaise, mustard, vinegar, and sugar. Pour over the cabbage mixture, season with salt and pepper, and toss to coat evenly.

Lay the bun bottoms, cut side up, on individual plates. Divide the chicken and sauce evenly among the bun bottoms and top with the slaw. Cap with the bun tops and serve.

SUMMER FAMILY BBQ

Oakville Potato Salad

Our signature potato salad is made with an herbaceous mixture of fresh dill, parsley, and green onions along with a big dose of Dijon mustard to add zing. Be sure to use waxy potatoes, which hold their shape better than their starchy cousins. For a particularly festive bowl, use a mix of red, yellow, purple, white, and/or blue potatoes.

MAKES 6 SERVINGS

3 lb small red or multicolored waxy potatoes, halved (or quartered if large)

Kosher salt and freshly ground pepper

3 tablespoons white balsamic vinegar

1 cup mayonnaise

¼ cup Dijon mustard, or to taste

4 celery ribs, finely chopped

3 green onions, white and green parts, thinly sliced

2 tablespoons finely chopped dill pickle (optional)

2 tablespoons finely chopped fresh flat-leaf parsley

2 tablespoons finely chopped fresh dill

Place the unpeeled potatoes in a large saucepan, add salted water to cover by 1 inch, cover the pan, and bring to a boil over high heat. Set the lid askew, reduce the heat to medium-low, and cook at a brisk simmer until the potatoes are tender, about 25 minutes. Drain, rinse the potatoes under cold running water until cooled, and drain again.

Transfer the potatoes to a sheet pan and season with salt. Sprinkle with the vinegar and toss to coat evenly. Let cool completely.

In a large bowl, stir together the mayonnaise and mustard. Add the potatoes, celery, green onions, dill pickle (if using), parsley, and dill and mix gently. Season with salt and pepper. Cover and refrigerate until chilled, at least 2 hours or up to overnight. Serve chilled.

Oakville Grocery | The Cookbook

SUMMER FAMILY BBQ

Grilled Corn, Tomato, and Roasted Pepper Salad with Cilantro

This grilled corn salad has all the flavors of Mexican elote, charred corn on the cob dressed with cheese and a spicy, citrusy sauce. We deconstruct that street food classic, mixing smoke-kissed corn kernels, cherry tomatoes, sweet peppers, cilantro, and Cotija cheese with an aromatic lime, garlic, and chile vinaigrette to create a salad you'll want to include at every barbecue.

MAKES 6–8 SERVINGS

Juice of 3 limes

2 teaspoons ground cumin

1 teaspoon mild chili powder

1 small clove garlic, minced

½ cup extra-virgin olive oil, plus more for brushing

Kosher salt and freshly ground pepper

6 ears corn, husks and silk removed

3 cups halved cherry tomatoes

½ cup diced jarred roasted red peppers

½ cup thinly sliced red onion

½ cup chopped fresh cilantro

¼ lb Cotija or feta cheese, crumbled

2 cups arugula

In a bowl, whisk together the lime juice, cumin, chili powder, and garlic. Pour in the oil in a slow, steady stream while whisking constantly to make a vinaigrette. Season with salt and pepper. Set aside.

Prepare a fire in a charcoal or gas grill for direct cooking over medium-high heat (400°F–450°F). Brush the grill grate clean. Brush a little oil on each ear of corn. Grill the corn, turning the ears often so they cook evenly, until lightly charred on all sides, about 10 minutes. Transfer to a work surface.

Using a sharp knife, cut the kernels off of each cob. Put the kernels into a large bowl. Add the tomatoes, roasted peppers, onion, cilantro, and cheese and toss to combine. Drizzle with some of the vinaigrette and toss to coat evenly. Add the arugula, toss again, and serve, passing the remaining dressing at the table.

Oakville Grocery | The Cookbook

SUMMER FAMILY BBQ

Cucumber-Lime Agua Fresca

Agua frescas are bright, refreshing drinks and make a terrific nonalcoholic option. Many are fruit based (or sometimes made with flowers or seeds), with water and sweetener added to taste. This invigorating lime and cucumber blend is particularly well received on a hot summer day. If you like, add a seeded and chopped serrano chile or a handful of fresh mint leaves to the blender.

MAKES 6 DRINKS

4½ cups water

10 Kirby cucumbers, peeled, halved lengthwise, seeded, and chopped

1 cup fresh lime juice

2 tablespoons agave nectar or honey

Pinch of kosher salt

Ice cubes, for serving

In a blender, working in batches, combine the water, cucumbers, lime juice, agave nectar, and salt and blend on high speed until smooth. Taste for sweetness and blend in more agave nectar if needed. Strain through a fine-mesh sieve into a pitcher. Refrigerate until chilled, at least 1 hour, before serving.

Fill glasses with ice, pour in the agua fresca, and serve.

SUMMER FAMILY BBQ

Triple–Chocolate Chip Cookie Ice Cream Sandwiches

This is two recipes in one: a triple–chocolate chip cookie and an ice cream sandwich. Make the cookies in advance and freeze them (if you can resist the temptation!), then sandwich them with your favorite ice cream the day you want to serve them. Vanilla is always a favorite, but have fun with other flavors, such as salted caramel, cookie dough, or coffee almond fudge.

MAKES 8 ICE CREAM SANDWICHES

For the cookies

½ cup unsalted butter, at room temperature

½ cup firmly packed light brown sugar

6 tablespoons granulated sugar

½ teaspoon kosher salt

1 large egg

1 teaspoon pure vanilla extract

1¼ cups all-purpose flour

1 teaspoon baking soda

1 cup semisweet chocolate chips

¼ cup white chocolate chips

¼ cup milk chocolate chips

1½ pints ice cream, flavor of your choice, slightly softened

To make the cookies, position 2 racks evenly in the oven and preheat the oven to 350°F. Line 2 sheet pans with parchment paper.

In a bowl, using an electric mixer, beat together the butter, both sugars, and the salt on medium speed until smooth and lightened. Add the egg and vanilla and beat until well blended. Add the flour and baking soda, and, using a wooden spoon, stir just until fully incorporated. Stir in all the chocolate chips.

For each cookie, drop a heaping tablespoon of the dough (a cookie scoop works well here) onto the prepared pans, spacing the cookies 2 inches apart. You should have at least 16 cookies.

Bake the cookies, switching the pans between the racks and rotating them back to front halfway through baking, until the bottoms and edges are lightly browned, 10–13 minutes. Gently press down on each cookie with a metal spatula as soon as they come out of the oven to flatten evenly.

Let the cookies cool on the pans on wire racks for 5 minutes, then transfer them to the racks to cool completely. (The cookies will keep in an airtight container at room temperature for up to 3 days.)

To make the ice cream sandwiches, place half of the cookies, bottom side up, on a work surface. Place a scoop of the ice cream (about ⅓ cup) on each cookie. Top with the remaining cookies, bottom side down, and gently press each sandwich to flatten the ice cream evenly. The ice cream should reach to the edge of the cookies. Place the sandwiches on a sheet pan and freeze for at least 1 hour before serving. (To keep the sandwiches longer, once they are frozen, slip them into a large resealable plastic freezer bag and store in the freezer for up to 3 weeks.)

Oakville Grocery | The Cookbook   95

LOCAL ARTISAN

MAD FRITZ BREWING CO.

We count Mad Fritz Brewery and Malthouse beers—brewed right up the street from Oakville Grocery in St. Helena—

as one of our favorite local additions to our beer selection. The owners, husband-and-wife team Nile Zacherle and Whitney Fisher, have been winemakers by trade for more than twenty years. But it was their love of home brewing that caused them to turn their passion into a business in 2012.

Starting with the equipment from their wineries, and using their knowledge of winemaking and home brewing, they developed a custom brewing system. Their unique beers are all barrel aged using locally grown single-malt barley and hops. They even named the brewery after their kids: Madeleine (Maddie) and Frederick (Fritz).

On the Mad Fritz website, Nile and Whitney explain how they have come to craft their singular lagers and ales: "Our combined experience in winemaking and brewing offers a unique landscape from where we can grow, malt, brew, and age beers with a sense of place and personality."

Each of the Mad Fritz products has a one-of-a-kind story and tasting notes, which makes it easy to select the perfect companion to your lunch or picnic.

PHOTOGRAPHS: JEFF BRAMWELL

CALIFORNIA COASTAL PICNIC

Peach and Prosciutto Flatbread

Sweet peaches, extra-creamy burrata, and salty prosciutto are a winning trifecta. You can roast the peaches in the oven up to a day in advance or, if your peaches are quite ripe and sweet, simply slice them thinly and place the slices directly onto the dough. This flatbread is also delicious topped with a few handfuls of arugula just before serving.

MAKES 1 FLATBREAD; 2–4 SERVINGS

One 8-oz ball pizza dough, homemade (page 205) or store-bought

1 tablespoon unsalted butter

1 firm but ripe peach or nectarine, preferably freestone, halved and pitted

Semolina or fine cornmeal, for dusting

1/4 lb burrata cheese

Olive oil, for brushing

2 oz thinly sliced prosciutto

Handful of fresh basil leaves, torn

Balsamic Glaze (page 210), for finishing (optional)

If using homemade dough, cover the dough ball and let come to room temperature for 4–6 hours; for store-bought dough, let the dough come to room temperature for 2–3 hours.

Preheat the oven to 425°F. In a small cast-iron frying pan over medium-high heat, melt the butter. Add the peach halves, cut side down, and cook until they start to brown, about 4 minutes. Transfer the pan to the oven and roast the peaches until just tender, about 10 minutes (the cooking time will depend on the ripeness of the fruit). Transfer the peach halves to a cutting board and let cool slightly, then thinly slice.

Position a rack in the upper third of the oven, about 6 inches from the heat source, and place a pizza stone on the rack. Raise the oven temperature to 550°F (or as high as your oven will go). Once the oven comes to temperature, let the stone continue to heat for 15 minutes longer.

When the oven and the stone are preheated, turn off the oven and turn on the broiler while you assemble the flatbread. On a lightly floured work surface, pull the dough into a thin round crust about 12 inches in diameter. Dust a pizza peel with semolina and slide the dough onto the peel. (If you don't have a peel, use a rimless cookie sheet or an inverted sheet pan.) Arrange the peach slices on the dough, then top with the burrata, adding it in evenly spaced clumps.

Turn off the broiler and return the oven temperature to 550°F. Carefully slide the flatbread onto the hot pizza stone and bake until the cheese is melted and the crust is golden brown, 6–8 minutes. Using the peel, remove from the oven and transfer to a cutting board. Immediately brush the edges of the dough with oil, then top the flatbread with the prosciutto and garnish with the basil. Drizzle with the balsamic glaze (if using), cut into pieces, and serve.

Oakville Grocery | The Cookbook

CALIFORNIA COASTAL PICNIC

Curry Chicken Salad with Avocado

This medium-spiced, slightly sweet, pleasantly creamy chicken salad is a star of our deli case. Serve it as a salad atop mixed greens with avocado and tomatoes, as we do at the store, or you can tuck it into a ciabatta or brioche roll with lettuce for a delicious sandwich. If you can't find Major Grey's chutney, substitute regular mango chutney and add 1 tablespoon fresh lime juice.

MAKES 6 SERVINGS

For the chicken salad

2 lb bone-in, skin-on chicken breast halves

½ yellow onion, cut into chunks

2 cloves garlic, smashed

½ cup dry white wine

1 tablespoon Madras curry powder

1 teaspoon ground turmeric

2 teaspoons kosher salt

½ teaspoon freshly ground pepper

1 large celery rib, finely chopped

2 green onions, white and green parts, thinly sliced

⅓ cup chopped roasted cashews

¼ cup packed shredded carrots

¼ cup chopped fresh flat-leaf parsley, plus more for garnish

3 tablespoons dried currants

For the dressing

½ cup mayonnaise

¼ cup plain yogurt or sour cream

3 tablespoons Major Grey's chutney

2½ teaspoons Madras curry powder

Kosher salt and freshly ground black pepper

To make the chicken salad, in a large saucepan, combine the chicken, yellow onion, garlic, wine, curry powder, turmeric, salt, and pepper. Add just enough water (2–3 cups) to cover the chicken. Bring to a gentle boil over medium-high heat, then reduce the heat to low, cover partially, and simmer gently until the chicken is cooked through, about 30 minutes, depending on the size of the breasts. Transfer the chicken to a cutting board and let cool.

Remove and discard the skin, bones, and any gristle from the chicken breasts and cut the meat into small bite-size pieces. You should have about 4 cups cooked chicken. Transfer the chicken to a large bowl and add the celery, green onions, cashews, carrots, parsley, and currants.

To make the dressing, in a small bowl, whisk together the mayonnaise, yogurt, chutney, and curry powder. Season with salt and pepper. Add the dressing to the chicken mixture and stir until evenly coated. Taste and adjust the flavors to your liking with more chutney, curry powder, salt, and pepper if needed.

To serve, in a bowl, toss the mixed greens with a drizzle of the vinaigrette. Divide the greens evenly among individual plates and top with the chicken salad. Arrange the avocado and tomato slices alongside the salad, dividing them evenly. Garnish the plates with parsley and serve.

Note: For serving, use 5 oz mixed salad greens (about 6 cups), ¼ cup Golden Balsamic Vinaigrette (page 214), 1 ripe avocado, halved, pitted, peeled, and thinly sliced, plus 1–2 large tomatoes, sliced.

CALIFORNIA COASTAL PICNIC

Summer Panzanella Salad

We clearly never tire of tomatoes in the summer months, and this is just another inspired way to use them. In this seasonal take on panzanella, the bread and tomatoes form the base of the salad, which is embellished with cucumber, onion, and basil and dressed with a garlic-shallot vinaigrette. In other seasons, use what is available. For example, in spring, omit the tomatoes and basil and add blanched asparagus, thinly sliced sugar snap peas, and fresh chives and tarragon.

MAKES 6 SERVINGS

6 heaping cups cubed country-style bread, such as ciabatta, in 1-inch cubes

2 tablespoons extra-virgin olive oil

2 large heirloom tomatoes, cut into bite-sized pieces

1 cup halved cherry tomatoes

Kosher salt and freshly ground pepper

1 small English cucumber, peeled, halved lengthwise, and sliced crosswise

1 small red onion, halved and very thinly sliced

1 cup fresh basil leaves, torn, plus small whole leaves for garnish

For the vinaigrette

1 small shallot, minced

1 small clove garlic, minced

1 teaspoon Dijon mustard

3 tablespoons red wine vinegar

⅓ cup extra-virgin olive oil

Kosher salt and freshly ground pepper

Preheat the oven to 375°F. Spread the bread cubes on a large sheet pan and drizzle evenly with the oil. Bake, turning once or twice, until lightly toasted, about 15 minutes. Set aside to cool.

While the bread toasts, in a large, fine-mesh sieve set over a bowl, toss the heirloom and cherry tomatoes with a large pinch of salt. Let sit for 10 minutes to drain. Transfer the tomatoes to a large serving bowl, reserving the tomato juice. Add the cucumber, onion, and torn basil to the tomatoes.

To make the vinaigrette, in a pint jar, combine the shallot, garlic, mustard, vinegar, and 3 tablespoons of the reserved tomato juice. Cap tightly and shake to mix well. Add the oil to the jar, cap tightly again, and shake vigorously to emulsify. Season with salt and pepper.

Add the toasted bread to the bowl with the tomato mixture and drizzle with half of the dressing. Toss the salad, then taste and adjust the seasoning with salt, pepper, and more dressing if needed. Garnish with the whole basil leaves and serve.

CALIFORNIA COASTAL PICNIC

Gazpacho

This chilled summer soup from Spain is most often made with tomatoes, as here, but there are many other variations out there—think cucumber, watermelon, and even almond. The beauty of this soup is that you can throw all the ingredients into the blender and voila!—lunch is made. When you have a bounty of overripe tomatoes, substitute 2 pounds fresh for the canned.

MAKES 2 QUARTS; ABOUT 8 SERVINGS

1 can (28 oz) crushed tomatoes or 2 lb fresh tomatoes, chopped

2 cups tomato juice

½ cup salsa

½ red bell pepper, seeded and finely chopped

½ green bell pepper, seeded and finely chopped

½ English cucumber, peeled, halved, seeded, and chopped

½ small yellow onion, finely chopped

1 clove garlic, chopped

¼ cup chopped fresh cilantro, plus more for garnish

¼ cup chopped fresh flat-leaf parsley

¼ cup extra-virgin olive oil

¼ cup red wine vinegar

Juice of 1 lemon

Grated zest and juice of 1 lime

1 tablespoon sugar

Kosher salt and freshly ground pepper

Garlic croutons, for garnish

2 avocados, halved, pitted, peeled, and diced, for garnish

In a large nonreactive bowl, combine the crushed tomatoes, tomato juice, tomato salsa, red and green bell peppers, cucumber, onion, garlic, cilantro, parsley, oil, vinegar, lemon juice, lime zest and juice, and sugar and mix well. In a blender, working in batches, purée the mixture until very smooth. As each batch is ready, transfer it to a second large bowl.

Season the soup with salt and pepper, then cover and refrigerate until well chilled and the flavors have married, at least 3 hours or up to overnight.

Just before serving, taste and adjust the seasoning with salt and pepper if needed. Ladle into bowls, garnish with the croutons, avocado, and cilantro, and serve chilled.

CALIFORNIA COASTAL PICNIC

Vegetable Romesco Sandwiches

This popular vegetable-packed sandwich has a little bit of everything, culminating in a wonderful combination of flavors and textures. Romesco, which originated in Catalonia Spain, is traditionally a rich, tangy puréed sauce of tomatoes, ñora peppers, garlic, olive oil, bread, vinegar, and almonds and/or hazelnuts. It's easy to make (our recipe uses jarred red peppers and no tomatoes), but you can also find good ready-made versions.

MAKES 2 SANDWICHES

1 teaspoon olive oil

1 small leek, white and light green parts, halved lengthwise and sliced crosswise

Kosher salt and freshly ground pepper

4 slices artisanal bread, such as Della Fattoria semolina bread

6 tablespoons romesco sauce, homemade (page 210) or store-bought

6 thin slices zucchini, cut lengthwise

6 thin slices cucumber, cut lengthwise

8 fresh basil leaves

½ cup drained and sliced piquillo peppers

1 cup alfalfa sprouts

2 tablespoons Balsamic Glaze (page 210)

In a small frying pan over medium-low heat, warm the oil. Add the leek, season with salt and pepper, and cook, stirring, until tender, about 3 minutes. Let cool.

Lay the bread slices on a cutting board. Spread one side of each slice with the romesco sauce, dividing it evenly. Divide the leeks evenly between 2 of the bread slices. Top each leek-covered bread slice with half each of the zucchini slices, cucumber slices, basil leaves, piquillo peppers, and sprouts, layering them evenly. Drizzle the sprouts with the balsamic glaze. Top with the remaining bread slices, cut each sandwich in half, and serve.

CALIFORNIA COASTAL PICNIC

Turkey, Bacon, and Tomato Sandwiches

Making a great sandwich—and using the best-quality ingredients—is something we take pride in doing for our customers, even one as commonplace as a turkey sandwich. At the store, if you ask for avocado in your turkey sandwich, we'll add some. You can do the same here: just pit, peel, and slice a small avocado and arrange half of the avocado slices on 2 of the aioli-topped bread slices, spreading them in an even layer. Gently press the avocado into the bread with a fork, then continue to build the sandwiches as directed.

MAKES 2 SANDWICHES

4 slices thick-cut bacon

2 ciabatta rolls, split

6 tablespoons Garlic Aioli (page 211)

6 oz roast turkey, such as Hobbs, thinly sliced

6 heirloom or beefsteak tomato slices

½ cup alfalfa sprouts

2 large leaves green leaf lettuce, torn to fit

In a frying pan over medium-low heat, cook the bacon, turning once or twice, until the fat renders and the bacon becomes crispy, about 8 minutes. Transfer to paper towels to drain.

Lay the roll halves, cut side up, on a cutting board. Spread with the aioli, dividing it evenly. Top each bottom half with half each of the turkey, bacon, tomato slices, sprouts, and lettuce, layering them evenly. Cap with the roll tops, cut each sandwich in half, and serve.

CALIFORNIA COASTAL PICNIC

Summer Berry Streusel Bars

Crumbly, buttery berry bars are always a welcome picnic option. For easy transport that also looks elegant, wrap each bar individually in parchment paper, securing it with decorative tape or kitchen string. If you like, use the homemade strawberry jam on page 70 for these bars.

MAKES 20 BARS

¾ cup cold unsalted butter, cut into chunks, plus room-temperature butter for the pan

1⅔ cups all-purpose flour

1 cup firmly packed light brown sugar

2 teaspoons pure vanilla extract

1 teaspoon ground cinnamon

½ teaspoon salt

¼ teaspoon baking soda

Finely grated zest of 1 small orange

1⅔ cups old-fashioned rolled oats

1½ cups mixed-berry jam

Preheat the oven to 350°F. Generously butter a 9-by-13-inch baking pan.

In a food processor, combine the flour, sugar, vanilla, cinnamon, salt, baking soda, and orange zest and pulse briefly to mix. Sprinkle the cold butter over the flour mixture and pulse until coarse crumbs form. Add the oats and pulse a few times to mix well.

Transfer about two-thirds of the oat mixture to the prepared pan and press firmly onto the bottom so it holds together. Using an offset spatula, spread the jam evenly over the top. Sprinkle the remaining oat mixture evenly over the jam to form a crumbly topping.

Bake until the top is golden and the jam is bubbling, 35–40 minutes. Let cool completely in the pan on a wire rack. Using a large knife, cut into 20 squares and carefully ease out of the pan to serve. Leftover bars will keep in an airtight container at room temperature for up to 4 days.

MENUS

FALL

Weekend Brunch with Friends

Autumn Harvest Picnic

Wine Country Cocktail Party

Fall Pizza Party

RECIPES

WEEKEND BRUNCH WITH FRIENDS
Autumn Fruit Salad with Honey Vinaigrette 112
Chorizo and Potato Breakfast Burritos 115
Vegetable Breakfast Burritos 116
Crunchy Cabbage Slaw 117
Mini Cinnamon-Sugar Muffins 120
Pineapple-Mint Mocktail 121

AUTUMN HARVEST PICNIC
Oakville Signature Salad with Grilled Chicken,
Blue Cheese, and Marcona Almonds 123
Cannellini Bean and Artichoke Salad 124
Muffaletta Sandwiches 125
Roast Beef Sandwiches with Olive Tapenade 126
Apple Spice Hand Pies 128

WINE COUNTRY COCKTAIL PARTY
Romesco and Skyhill Chèvre Flatbread 129
Bite-Size Dungeness Crab Cakes 131
Oysters with Citrus-Chile Mignonette 132
Tri-Tip Sandwich Sliders 133
BLT Deviled Eggs 134
Mt Tam Cheese and Bacon Jam Crostini 136
Pomegranate Gin Fizz 137
Passion Fruit–Blood Orange Kiss 139
Apple Bourbon Old-Fashioned 140

FALL PIZZA PARTY
Wild Mushroom, Caramelized Onion, and
Goat Cheese Pizza 145
Mascarpone, Speck, and Arugula Pizza 146
Spicy Sausage, Tomato, and Fontina Pizza 147
Thai Crunch Mezzaluna 150
Yogurt Panna Cotta with Fresh Figs 151
Bitter Greens Salad with Pear and Toasted Walnuts 152

WEEKEND BRUNCH WITH FRIENDS

Autumn Fruit Salad with Honey Vinaigrette

You can create a fruit salad with virtually any combination of fruits, but the savviest choices will bring together the best of the season, like this autumn-inspired mix of apples, pears, grapes, tangerines, and pecans. At the store, our summer version is made with strawberries, blueberries, blackberries, green and red grapes, and sometimes fresh mint. Have fun experimenting with your favorite seasonal fruits.

MAKES 6 SERVINGS

2 tablespoons rice vinegar

2 teaspoons honey

¼ cup extra-virgin olive oil

3 pears, about 1 lb total, halved, cored, and diced

2 tart-sweet green or red apples, halved, cored, and diced

2 cups red and/or green seedless grapes (about ¾ lb)

1 cup chopped tangerine segments

½ cup pomegranate seeds

¼ cup chopped pecans or walnuts, toasted (optional)

In a small bowl, whisk together the vinegar, honey, and oil until blended to make a vinaigrette.

In a large, wide serving bowl, combine the pears, apples, grapes, tangerine, and pomegranate seeds. Drizzle with the vinaigrette and toss gently to coat evenly. Garnish with the pecans (if using) and serve.

WEEKEND BRUNCH WITH FRIENDS

Chorizo and Potato Breakfast Burritos

The classic pairing of Mexican-style chorizo and potatoes is excellent in these generously loaded breakfast burritos. If you like, add sliced avocado or pico de gallo before you roll up each burrito. To serve a group, double the recipe and assemble the burritos just before everyone arrives, then wrap them in foil, line them up on a sheet pan, and slip the pan into a 200°F oven so they stay warm.

MAKES 4 BURRITOS

¾ lb small Yukon Gold potatoes, cut into ½-inch pieces

3 tablespoons olive oil

Kosher salt and freshly ground pepper

¾ lb fresh Mexican-style chorizo, casings removed

½ small yellow onion, finely chopped

1 small red bell pepper, seeded and diced

1 jalapeño chile, seeded and minced (optional)

1 clove garlic, minced

3 tablespoons chopped fresh cilantro or oregano

8 large eggs

2 tablespoons milk or water

2 tablespoons unsalted butter

4 flour tortillas, each about 9 inches in diameter, warmed

1 cup shredded Cheddar cheese

Salsa and sour cream, for serving

Fill a large saucepan half full of salted water, add the potatoes, and bring to a boil over medium-high heat. Cook, stirring occasionally, until just crisp-tender, about 7 minutes. Drain well in a fine-mesh sieve.

In a frying pan over medium heat, warm 1 tablespoon of the oil. Add the potatoes, season with salt and pepper, and cook, stirring, until the potatoes are browned and tender, about 5 minutes. Transfer to a bowl.

Add 1 tablespoon of the oil to the pan. Crumble the chorizo into the pan and cook, breaking up the chorizo with the side of a wooden spoon, until it browns, about 8 minutes. Using a slotted spoon, transfer to the bowl with the potatoes. Pour off any fat in the pan.

Warm the remaining 1 tablespoon oil in the pan. Add the onion, bell pepper, jalapeño (if using), and garlic, and cook, stirring frequently, until the onion is tender, about 5 minutes. Return the chorizo and potatoes to the pan and cook, stirring, until the mixture is well mixed and warmed through. Season with salt and pepper and stir in the cilantro. Remove from the heat and cover to keep warm.

In a bowl, whisk together the eggs, milk, ½ teaspoon salt, and ¼ teaspoon pepper. In a nonstick frying pan over medium-low heat, melt the butter. Add the eggs and cook, stirring occasionally, until just cooked through but still moist, 3–4 minutes.

To assemble the burritos, lay the warm tortillas on a work surface. Divide the eggs evenly among the tortillas, spooning them onto the bottom half of each tortilla and leaving a 1½-inch border uncovered. Sprinkle the cheese over the eggs, dividing it evenly. Top with the chorizo mixture, again dividing it evenly. Fold in both sides of a tortilla about 1 inch, then, starting at the bottom, lift the bottom edge up and over the filling, snugly tucking it just under the filling, and continue to roll to the far edge. Repeat with the remaining tortillas and filling. Serve with the salsa and sour cream alongside.

Oakville Grocery | The Cookbook   115

WEEKEND BRUNCH WITH FRIENDS

Vegetable Breakfast Burritos

Stuffed with eggs and plenty of vegetables, this warm breakfast burrito can't be beat for a casual brunch or an early-morning meal on the go, especially when you need something hearty. We make a few combinations, such as the potatoes, mushrooms, and spinach used here and a summer favorite that includes grilled or sautéed eggplant, bell peppers, and zucchini. Change up these combinations with whatever vegetables you like to create your own ideal vegetable burrito.

MAKES 4 BURRITOS

¾ lb small Yukon Gold potatoes, cut into ½-inch pieces

3 tablespoons olive oil

Kosher salt and freshly ground pepper

½ small yellow onion, finely chopped

½ lb cremini mushrooms, brushed clean, stem ends trimmed, and sliced

5 oz baby spinach (about 4 cups)

3 tablespoons chopped fresh cilantro or oregano

8 large eggs

2 tablespoons milk or water

1 tablespoon unsalted butter

4 flour tortillas, each about 9 inches in diameter, warmed

1 cup shredded Cheddar cheese

Salsa and sour cream, for serving

Fill a large saucepan half full of salted water, add the potatoes, and bring to a boil over medium-high heat. Cook, stirring occasionally, until just crisp-tender, about 7 minutes. Drain well in a fine-mesh sieve.

In a large nonstick frying pan over medium heat, warm 1 tablespoon of the oil. Add the potatoes, season with salt and pepper, and cook, stirring, until the potatoes are browned and tender, about 5 minutes. Transfer to a large bowl.

Add 1 tablespoon of the oil to the pan. Add the onion and cook, stirring, until golden brown, about 8 minutes. Add the mushrooms, season with salt and pepper, and cook, stirring, until they are tender and dry, about 5 minutes. Add the spinach and cook, stirring, until wilted and the liquid has evaporated, about 3 minutes. Stir in the cilantro and remove from the heat. Transfer to the bowl with the potatoes and toss to mix. Wipe out the pan.

In a bowl, whisk together the eggs, milk, ½ teaspoon salt, and ¼ teaspoon pepper. Return the frying pan to medium-low heat and add the remaining 1 tablespoon oil and the butter. When the butter melts, add the eggs and cook, stirring occasionally, until just cooked through but still moist, 3-4 minutes.

To assemble the burritos, lay the warm tortillas on a work surface. Divide the eggs evenly among the tortillas, spooning them onto the bottom half of each tortilla and leaving a 1 ½-inch border uncovered. Sprinkle the cheese over the eggs, dividing it evenly. Top with the mushroom-spinach-potato mixture, again dividing it evenly. Fold in both sides of a tortilla about 1 inch, then, starting at the bottom, lift the bottom edge up and over the filling, snugly tucking it just under the filling, and continue to roll to the far edge. Repeat with the remaining tortillas and filling. Serve with the salsa and sour cream alongside.

WEEKEND BRUNCH WITH FRIENDS

Crunchy Cabbage Slaw

Cabbage, celery, apple, and carrots deliver a lot of crunch to this creamy coleslaw, while a little chopped parsley and a bit of lemon juice add fresh flavor. This is also a great side dish just about any time you are looking for an easy, make-ahead salad to accompany barbecued or grilled meats and poultry—or to set alongside Francisco's Fried Chicken Tenders (page 44).

MAKES 6 SERVINGS

1 small head green cabbage, about 1½ lb, cored and finely shredded

2 celery ribs, diced

1 Granny Smith apple, cored and shredded

½ small red onion, very finely chopped

2 small carrots, peeled and shredded

2 tablespoons finely chopped fresh flat-leaf parsley

¾ cup mayonnaise, homemade (page 210) or store-bought

2 tablespoons fresh lemon juice

2 tablespoons cider vinegar, plus more as needed

1–2 tablespoons sugar

Kosher salt and freshly ground pepper

In a large bowl, toss together the cabbage, celery, apple, onion, carrots, and parsley.

In a small bowl, whisk together the mayonnaise, lemon juice, vinegar, and sugar to taste. Pour over the cabbage mixture and toss to coat evenly. Season with salt and pepper. Cover and refrigerate until chilled, at least 2 hours or up to 8 hours.

Just before serving, taste and adjust the seasoning with vinegar, salt, and pepper if needed. Serve chilled.

Oakville Grocery | The Cookbook   117

LOCAL ARTISAN

RANCHO GORDO

Rancho Gordo started with Steve Sando's frustration with not being able to find fresh, ripe, flavorful tomatoes.

Based in the wine country town of Napa, Steve began growing his own tomatoes. This led to experimenting with beans . . . and, well, the rest is history. After growing—and cooking—all sorts of heirloom beans, and marveling at their nuanced flavors, Steve set up a table at the local farmers' market. The business immediately took off. Nowadays, the ubiquitous brand is synonymous with quality heirloom beans, corn, grains, spices, and more—many ingredients native to the Americas.

On the company website, Steve describes why he became a bean farmer: "All of my agricultural pursuits have been based on being someone who likes to cook but gets frustrated by the lack of ingredients, especially those that are native to the Americas. One of the things that originally drew me to beans was the fact that they are indigenous to the Americas. It seems to me these indigenous ingredients should be familiar, if not common."

The business makes its home in Napa but has expanded to grow its products in Central California, along the West Coast, and in New Mexico. Rancho Gordo also works with small farms in Mexico that raise rare heirloom crops.

PHOTOGRAPHS: LEFT: KIM SERVEAU; RIGHT: STEVE SANDO

WEEKEND BRUNCH WITH FRIENDS

Mini Cinnamon-Sugar Muffins

Lightly spiced buttermilk muffins are delicately sweet on their own, but when brushed with melted butter and dredged in plenty of cinnamon sugar, they take on a whole new personality reminiscent of churros. To make standard-size muffins, grease a 12-cup standard muffin pan, fill each cup about two-thirds full, and add a few minutes to the baking time.

MAKES ABOUT 40 MINI MUFFINS

Cooking spray, for the pans

1½ cups all-purpose flour

1½ teaspoons baking powder

½ teaspoon baking soda

½ teaspoon kosher salt

½ teaspoon ground cinnamon

⅛ teaspoon freshly grated nutmeg

4 tablespoons unsalted butter, at room temperature

¼ cup canola or avocado oil

⅔ cup sugar

1 large egg

2 teaspoons pure vanilla extract

½ cup buttermilk

For the topping

⅔ cup sugar

1 tablespoon ground cinnamon

6 tablespoons unsalted butter, melted

Preheat the oven to 375°F. Grease two 24-cup mini muffin pans with cooking spray.

In a medium bowl, whisk together the flour, baking powder, baking soda, salt, cinnamon, and nutmeg. In a large bowl, using an electric mixer, beat together the butter, oil, and sugar on medium speed until light and fluffy. Add the egg and vanilla and beat until pale and smooth. Pour in the buttermilk and beat until well mixed. On low speed, add the flour mixture and beat just until evenly moistened. The batter may be slightly lumpy.

Spoon the batter into the prepared muffin cups, filling each three-fourths full (a 1-tablespoon scoop works well for this). Not all of the cups will be used. Bake the muffins until lightly golden and a toothpick inserted into the center of a muffin comes out clean, about 14 minutes. Let cool in the pans on wire racks for 5 minutes, then turn out the muffins onto the racks and let stand until cool enough to handle.

While the muffins cool, make the topping. In a small, shallow bowl, stir together the sugar and cinnamon. Put the butter into a second small bowl. Holding a warm muffin upside down, dip the top into the butter, turning the muffin to coat the top evenly. Then immediately dip the top in the cinnamon-sugar mixture, coating it evenly and tapping to remove the excess. Return the muffin, right side up, to a rack. Repeat with the remaining muffins.

Serve warm or at room temperature. Leftover muffins will keep in an airtight container at room temperature for up to 4 days.

WEEKEND BRUNCH WITH FRIENDS

Pineapple-Mint Mocktail

Pineapple, lime, and mint have a natural affinity to one another, so it's only fitting that we decided to transform them into this delicious mocktail influenced by two popular Caribbean cocktails, the mojito and rum punch. To turn this tropical sipper into a cocktail, add 3–4 ounces white rum to the lime juice mixture.

MAKES 4 MOCKTAILS

Ice cubes, for serving

20 fresh mint leaves, plus 4 sprigs for garnish

4 oz Simple Syrup (page 215)

4 oz fresh lime juice (from about 4 limes)

4 oz pineapple juice

12 oz sparkling water, or as needed

4 fresh pineapple wedges, for garnish

Fill 4 highball glasses with ice. In a mixing glass or small pitcher, combine the mint leaves and simple syrup. Using a muddler or pestle, gently muddle the mint leaves, being careful not to tear them. Stir in the lime juice and pineapple juice.

Fill the glasses about two-thirds full with the mixture, being sure to get a few mint leaves into each glass. Add the sparkling water, leaving a little room at the top of each glass, and stir gently. Garnish each drink with a mint sprig and a pineapple wedge and serve.

AUTUMN HARVEST PICNIC

Oakville Signature Salad with Grilled Chicken, Blue Cheese, and Marcona Almonds

The combination of grilled chicken, apples, almonds, currants, and blue cheese conjures up one of our favorite times of year: harvest season! When the wine grapes ripen, the leaves start to change color, and the nights begin to cool, we know the busiest time of year has arrived for our many friends at the surrounding wineries. This salad is easy to pack for a picnic: grill the chicken and tuck it, the vinaigrette, and the remaining salad ingredients into separate containers, then combine them when ready to serve. We like to use Point Reyes Original Blue for this flavorful salad.

MAKES 4 SERVINGS

1 lb boneless, skinless chicken breast halves

Fine sea salt and freshly ground pepper

1¼ cups Golden Balsamic Vinaigrette (page 214)

Olive oil

6 cups mixed salad greens

1 Granny Smith apple, halved, cored, and thinly sliced

½ small red onion, very thinly sliced

¼ cup roasted Marcona almonds or chopped toasted walnuts

2 tablespoons dried currants

¼ lb blue cheese, crumbled

Using a meat mallet, lightly pound each chicken breast to an even thickness of ¾–1 inch. Season the chicken all over with salt and pepper. Arrange in a single layer in a shallow baking dish, drizzle with ¼ cup of the dressing, and turn to coat evenly. Cover and refrigerate for at least 30 minutes or up to 2 hours.

Prepare a fire in a charcoal or gas grill for direct cooking over medium heat (350°F–400°F). Brush the grill grate clean and then oil the grate. Remove the chicken from the marinade, letting any excess marinade drip off. Grill the chicken, with the lid closed, until it releases easily from the grate, about 4 minutes. Turn and grill the other side until opaque all the way through, about 4 minutes longer. Set aside to cool for at least 10 minutes. Chop into bite-size pieces.

In a large, wide serving bowl, toss together the greens, apple, onion, almonds, and currants. Add the chicken and ¼ cup of the dressing and toss to coat evenly. Sprinkle with the blue cheese. Serve with the remaining dressing alongside.

AUTUMN HARVEST PICNIC

Cannellini Bean and Artichoke Salad

This piquant Italian-inspired bean and artichoke salad is a snap to put together if you use canned beans (or cook your beans the night before in an Instant Pot!). Make sure to let the salad stand for a while before serving so the beans soak up all the lemony goodness from the vinaigrette.

MAKES 6 SERVINGS

2 cans (15 oz each) cannellini beans, drained and rinsed

1 can (14 oz) artichoke hearts, drained and chopped

½ small red onion, finely chopped

2 celery ribs, diced

1 tablespoon finely chopped fresh oregano leaves

½ cup Lemon Vinaigrette (page 213), plus more for serving (optional)

Kosher salt and freshly ground pepper

In a large bowl, combine the beans, artichoke hearts, onion, celery, and oregano and toss to mix well. Drizzle with the vinaigrette, season with salt and pepper, and toss to coat evenly. Let stand for at least 30 minutes or cover and refrigerate for up to 4 hours to allow the flavors to blend.

Serve at room temperature, passing more vinaigrette alongside if desired.

AUTUMN HARVEST PICNIC

Muffaletta Sandwiches

Created by Sicilian immigrants living in New Orleans, the muffaletta is a hefty sandwich made with layers of thinly sliced Italian cold cuts and cheese on sesame bread. But it's the "olive salad," a chopped mixture of green and black olives, roasted red peppers, celery, peperoncini, and pickled cauliflower, onion, and carrot, that makes it truly special. It is sometimes called muffaletta mix and can be found in most well-stocked supermarkets. We add chile aioli and tapenade to our muffaletta, which takes this French Quarter staple to the next level.

MAKES 2 SANDWICHES

Two 8-inch lengths rustic baguette or 2 ciabatta rolls, split

½ cup store-bought olive salad (muffaletta mix), with oil for spreading

¼ cup Fresno Chile Aioli (page 211)

¼ cup black olive tapenade, homemade (page 209) or store-bought

¼ lb thinly sliced prosciutto

¼ lb thinly sliced mortadella

¼ lb thinly sliced salami, preferably wine cured

4 slices provolone cheese

Lay the baguette halves, cut side up, on a work surface. Brush with oil from the olive salad, then spread with the chile aioli, dividing it evenly. Spread each bottom half with half of the tapenade and top with half of the olive salad. Layer the prosciutto, mortadella, salami, and provolone on top of the tapenade, dividing them evenly. Cap each sandwich with the top half.

Cut in half and serve at once, grill on a panini press, or wrap tightly in plastic wrap and refrigerate overnight to allow the flavors to develop, then serve at room temperature.

To grill the sandwiches, preheat an electric panini press on medium-low according to the manufacturer's instructions. Place the sandwiches, one at a time, on the preheated press and cook according to the manufacturer's instructions until the sandwich is warmed through and the cheese is melted, 6–8 minutes.

Transfer the sandwiches to a cutting board, cut in half, and serve.

AUTUMN HARVEST PICNIC

Roast Beef Sandwiches with Olive Tapenade

This isn't your typical roast beef sandwich. We skip the usual horseradish, mustard, and cheese in favor of bright California flavors—basil aioli, briny olive tapenade, thick slices of late-season tomatoes—all piled high with thin slices of roast beef. For sliders, divide the fillings among mini ciabatta rolls, then wrap them individually in parchment paper and secure with kitchen string for safe picnic transport.

MAKES 2 SANDWICHES

4 large slices artisanal bread, such as Della Fattoria semolina bread

6 tablespoons Basil Aioli (page 211)

4 tablespoons black olive tapenade, homemade (page 209) or store-bought

6 oz thinly sliced roast beef, preferably Hobbs

6 thin tomato slices

4 thinly shaved red onion slices

1 cup mixed salad greens

Lay the bread slices on a cutting board. Spread one side of each bread slice with the aioli, dividing it evenly. Spread 2 of the bread slices with the tapenade, dividing it evenly. Top each tapenade-covered bread slice with half each of the roast beef, tomato, onion, and greens, layering them evenly. Top with the remaining bread slices, cut each sandwich in half, and serve.

AUTUMN HARVEST PICNIC

Apple Spice Hand Pies

The sweet spice–laden aroma of apple pie baking is a sure sign of autumn. And these small, round hand pies will not disappoint. Plus, they are the perfect size to pack for a picnic. Make, roll out, and cut, and refrigerate the dough the day before baking and these will be a snap to make. If you like, swap out the apples for pears.

MAKES 4 HAND PIES

3 tablespoons granulated sugar

2 tablespoons water

1 lb tart-sweet baking apples, such as Granny Smith or Honeycrisp, peeled, halved, cored, and cut into 1/8-inch-thick slices

1/2 teaspoon ground cinnamon

Pinch of freshly grated nutmeg

Pinch of kosher salt

1 teaspoon fresh lemon juice

Tart Dough (page 207)

1 large egg beaten with 1 teaspoon water

Turbinado sugar, for sprinkling

Vanilla ice cream, for serving

In a large sauté pan over medium heat, combine the granulated sugar and water and cook, stirring, until the sugar dissolves. Add the apples, cinnamon, nutmeg, and salt and cook, stirring occasionally, until the apples are just tender and the liquid is slightly thickened, 6–8 minutes. Transfer to a bowl and stir in the lemon juice. Let cool to room temperature.

On a lightly floured work surface, roll out the dough into a round about 1/8 inch thick. Using a 4½-inch round pastry or cookie cutter, cut out as many rounds as possible. Transfer the rounds to a sheet pan. Gather up the dough scraps, press them together, roll out, and cut out more rounds to total 8 rounds. Cover with plastic wrap and refrigerate for about 10 minutes before assembling the pies.

Preheat the oven to 400°F. Line a large sheet pan with parchment paper.

Arrange 4 dough rounds on the prepared pan, spacing them at least 1 inch apart. Brush the rounds with a little of the egg mixture, then place about ¼ cup of the apple filling in the center of each round. Lay a dough round over each apple-topped round, press the top and bottom edges together, and then crimp the edges with fork tines. Brush the top of each pie with the egg mixture. Cut a few small steam vents in the top of each pie. Sprinkle the tops lightly with turbinado sugar.

Bake the pies until the crust is golden brown, 18–22 minutes. Let cool on the pan on a wire rack for at least 15 minutes. Serve warm or at room temperature with a scoop of vanilla ice cream. The pies will keep in an airtight container at room temperature for up to 1 week.

WINE COUNTRY COCKTAIL PARTY

Romesco and Skyhill Chèvre Flatbread

With only two toppings, this flatbread might seem overly simple, but both the romesco sauce and the fresh goat cheese pack a flavor punch. For bite-size pieces perfect for a cocktail party, shape the dough into a rectangle, then cut the flatbread into two-bite squares.

MAKES 1 FLATBREAD

One 8-oz ball pizza dough, homemade (page 205) or store-bought

Semolina or fine cornmeal, for dusting

¼ cup romesco sauce, homemade (page 210) or store-bought

¼ lb Skyhill chèvre or other fresh goat cheese

Olive oil, for brushing

If using homemade dough, cover the dough ball and let come to room temperature for 4–6 hours; for store-bought dough, let the dough come to room temperature for 2–3 hours.

About 30 minutes before you are ready to bake the flatbread, position a rack in the upper third of the oven, about 6 inches from the heat source, and place a pizza stone on the rack. Preheat the oven to 550°F (or as high as your oven will go). Once the oven comes to temperature, let the stone continue to heat for 15 minutes longer.

When the oven and the stone are preheated, turn off the oven and turn on the broiler while you assemble the flatbread. On a lightly floured work surface, pull the dough into a thin round crust about 12 inches in diameter. Dust a pizza peel with semolina and slide the dough onto the peel. (If you don't have a peel, use a rimless cookie sheet or an inverted sheet pan.) Spread the romesco over the dough, then crumble the cheese evenly over the top.

Turn off the broiler and return the oven temperature to 550°F. Carefully slide the flatbread onto the hot pizza stone and bake until the crust is golden brown, 6–8 minutes. Using the peel, remove from the oven and transfer to a cutting board. Immediately brush the edges of the dough with oil. Cut into wedges and serve.

WINE COUNTRY COCKTAIL PARTY

Bite-Size Dungeness Crab Cakes

Here in Northern California, we eagerly await Dungeness crab season in late fall, when the local catch becomes available in markets. These bite-size crab cakes showcase the buttery, sweet, delicate flavor of this prized crustacean. We like to serve them with lemon aioli, but our chile aioli (page 211) or another of our flavored mayonnaises would also work well. If you prefer larger cakes, use a 2-tablespoon scoop to shape them.

MAKES ABOUT 24 SMALL CRAB CAKES

1 tablespoon unsalted butter

1 shallot, minced

½ red bell pepper, seeded and diced

1 Fresno chile, seeded and minced

1 small clove garlic, minced

1 teaspoon finely chopped fresh thyme leaves

¼ teaspoon ground mustard

⅛ teaspoon smoked paprika

⅛ teaspoon Old Bay Seasoning

Finely grated zest and juice of 1 lemon

2 tablespoons all-purpose flour

½ cup heavy cream

1 lb fresh-cooked lump crabmeat

1 large egg, lightly beaten

2 teaspoons finely chopped fresh chives

1 teaspoon finely chopped fresh flat-leaf parsley leaves

1½ cups panko or fine dried bread crumbs

Canola oil, for frying

Lemon wedges, for serving

Lemon Aioli (page 212), for serving

Line a sheet pan with parchment paper.

In a large frying pan over medium heat, melt the butter. Add the shallot, bell pepper, and chile and cook, stirring, until softened, about 5 minutes. Add the garlic, thyme, mustard, paprika, Old Bay, and lemon juice and cook gently, stirring, for 1 minute. Add the flour and cook, stirring, for 2 minutes. Add the cream and simmer, stirring, for 2 minutes. Transfer the mixture to a large bowl and let cool completely. Wipe out the pan.

Pick over the crabmeat for shell shards and cartilage. Add the crabmeat, egg, lemon zest, chives, and parsley to the cooled cream mixture and stir gently to mix. Add ½ cup of the panko and stir gently just until evenly blended; do not overmix.

Scoop up a large tablespoonful of the crab mixture for each cake (a 1-tablespoon scoop works well for this) and press gently into a ball. Transfer to the prepared sheet pan. You should have about 24 cakes total.

Pour the remaining 1 cup panko into a shallow bowl. One at a time, press the cakes into the panko, coating the entire surface lightly, and flattening them slightly. Return to the sheet pan.

Return the frying pan to the stove top and pour in oil to a depth of ½ inch. Warm over medium-high heat to 350°F on a deep-frying thermometer. Line a large sheet pan with paper towels.

Working in batches to avoid overcrowding, fry the crab cakes, turning once, until golden brown, about 4 minutes total. Using a slotted spatula, transfer the cakes to the paper towel–lined sheet pan to drain.

Serve the crab cakes hot with the lemon wedges and aioli on the side.

WINE COUNTRY COCKTAIL PARTY

Oysters with Citrus-Chile Mignonette

A platter of local oysters on the half shell adds elegance to any party. A classic mignonette sauce is a mixture of vinegar and shallot, but here we've given the dipping sauce a Napa Valley spin with the addition of lemon juice and minced Fresno chile. Oysters are best shucked and served the day you purchase them. Be sure to keep them well chilled until serving.

MAKES 36 OYSTERS

For the mignonette sauce

½ cup rice vinegar

1 large shallot, minced

1 Fresno chile, seeded and minced

1 teaspoon finely grated lemon zest

1 tablespoon fresh lemon juice

Freshly cracked pepper

Crushed or shaved ice, for the platter

36 oysters in the shell

Lemon wedges, for garnish

To make the sauce, in a small serving bowl, stir together the vinegar, shallot, chile, and lemon zest and juice. Season with pepper, then taste and add more vinegar or lemon juice if needed.

Place the bowl of sauce on a large platter and surround it with a bed of ice. Discard any oysters that do not close tightly to the touch. Scrub each oyster thoroughly with a stiff-bristled brush, rinsing it well under cold running water. Holding an oyster flat side up in a kitchen towel with your nondominant hand and using an oyster knife in your dominant hand, slip the tip of the knife into the shell near the hinge and twist and then pry upward to open. Run the knife blade along the inside of the top shell to sever the muscle that joins the shells, then lift off the top shell. Run the knife underneath the oyster to free it from the rounded bottom shell, being careful not to spill the liquor. Nest the oyster in its bottom shell on the ice. Repeat with the remaining oysters. Serve with the mignonette sauce and lemon wedges alongside.

WINE COUNTRY COCKTAIL PARTY

Tri-Tip Sandwich Sliders

We cook our tri-tip in the wood-fired pizza oven at the Oakville store. The smokiness from the wood gives the meat an irresistible fragrance, and we serve it on ciabatta with a smear of romesco sauce and a few pickle slices. You can replicate this at home on a charcoal or gas grill using wood chips. Popular in California, tri-tip is a triangular cut from the sirloin; we use Niman Ranch beef, but any good-quality beef will work.

MAKES 6–8 SERVINGS

For the smoked tri-tip

1 tri-tip roast, about 2 lb

1 tablespoon chili powder

2 teaspoons freshly ground pepper

1 teaspoon garlic powder

1 teaspoon kosher salt

About 4 cups wood chips, soaked in water for 30 minutes

Canola oil, for the grill grate

For the sliders

12 mini ciabatta rolls or slider buns, split

Romesco sauce, homemade (page 210) or store-bought, for spreading

Dijon mayonnaise, for spreading

Dill pickle slices

To make the tri-tip, about 1 hour before you are ready to grill, remove the tri-tip from the refrigerator. In a small bowl, stir together the chili powder, pepper, garlic powder, and salt. Season the tri-tip all over with the spice mixture and let come to room temperature.

Prepare a fire in a charcoal or gas grill for direct and indirect cooking over medium heat (350°F–400°F). If using charcoal, bank the lit coals on one side of the grill. Place a drip pan on the side without the coals and fill the pan with water. Add about 2 cups of the wood chips to the lit charcoal just before grilling. If using gas, fill a smoker box with up to 2 cups of the wood chips, then preheat the grill. Turn off a burner or two to create a cooler zone. Brush the grill grate clean and then oil the grate.

Place the tri-tip on the grill over direct heat and sear, turning as needed, until nicely browned but not charred on all sides, 10–15 minutes. Move the roast to the indirect heat, cover the grill, and cook for 15–30 minutes for medium-rare or to your desired doneness. Cooking times will vary depending on the size and shape of the roast. Remove the roast when an instant-read thermometer inserted into the thickest part of the meat registers 130°F for medium-rare or 135°F for medium.

Transfer the roast to a cutting board, cover loosely with aluminum foil, and let rest for 15 minutes. Slice very thinly against the grain, capturing any released juices. Transfer to a plate.

To assemble the sliders, lay the roll halves, cut side up, on a work surface. Spread with the romesco and then the dijonnaise. Top the bottom halves with the tri-tip and then the pickle slices. Cap with the roll tops, arrange the sliders on a platter or board, and serve.

Oakville Grocery | The Cookbook

WINE COUNTRY COCKTAIL PARTY

BLT Deviled Eggs

We love a straightforward deviled egg (see our recipe on page 85), but we also like to get creative with the classics. Here we add sun-dried tomatoes, crispy bacon, and chives for an over-the-top rendition of this much-loved cocktail party fare. If you like, cut a few extra slices of bacon into 1-inch pieces (you'll need 24 pieces total), fry until crispy, and garnish each deviled egg with a piece.

MAKES 24 STUFFED EGGS

3 slices thick-cut bacon, finely chopped

12 large eggs

½ cup mayonnaise

2 tablespoons country or regular Dijon mustard

¼ cup drained and minced oil-packed sun-dried tomatoes

2 tablespoons finely chopped fresh chives

1 tablespoon cider vinegar

¼ teaspoon kosher salt

¼ teaspoon freshly ground pepper

Sweet paprika, for sprinkling

In a frying pan over medium-low heat, cook the bacon, stirring occasionally, until the fat renders and the bacon becomes crispy, about 8 minutes. Transfer to paper towels to drain.

Meanwhile, boil the eggs. Have ready a large bowl of ice water. Fill a large saucepan half full of water and bring to a boil over high heat. Using a slotted spoon, carefully add the eggs to the boiling water. Reduce the heat to medium so the water is at a gentle boil and cook the eggs for 11 minutes.

Using the slotted spoon, transfer the eggs to the ice water. Let sit for 10 minutes. Then gently crack each egg against a work surface, rolling it back and forth under your hand, to crack the shell finely all over. Peel off the shell. Cut each egg in half lengthwise.

Using a spoon, scoop the yolks out of the egg whites into a bowl. Place the egg-white halves, hollow side up, on a serving platter. Add the mayonnaise, mustard, tomatoes, chives, vinegar, salt, and pepper to the yolks and, using a fork, mash them to a smooth, fluffy paste. Stir in the reserved bacon.

Spoon the yolk mixture into the egg-white halves, dividing it evenly and shaping it into a mound. Sprinkle each mound with a pinch of paprika and serve. The eggs can be made and refrigerated for up to 8 hours in advance before serving.

WINE COUNTRY COCKTAIL PARTY

Mt Tam Cheese and Bacon Jam Crostini

Once you make this bacon "jam," you'll want to put it on just about everything—from burgers to grilled cheese sandwiches. Here we showcase it on crunchy crostini with our favorite Cowgirl Creamery cheese, the extra-creamy Mt Tam. You can make the jam well in advance, so once it's party time, it's easy to assemble the crostini while you pour yourself a glass of wine.

MAKES 6 SERVINGS

For the bacon jam

1 lb thick-cut bacon, finely chopped

1 yellow onion, finely chopped

2 cloves garlic, minced

½ cup brewed strong coffee

¼ cup pure maple syrup

¼ cup firmly packed light brown sugar

3 tablespoons cider vinegar

Kosher salt and freshly ground pepper

For the crostini

Extra-virgin olive oil, for brushing

1 baguette, cut crosswise into ¼-inch-thick slices

Kosher salt and coarsely ground pepper

½ lb Cowgirl Creamery Mt Tam or other triple cream cheese, thinly sliced

To make the bacon jam, in a large, heavy frying pan over medium-low heat, cook the bacon, stirring occasionally, until the fat renders and the bacon begins to brown (but not crisp), about 8 minutes. Using a slotted spoon, transfer to paper towels to drain. Pour the fat into a small heatproof bowl and return 3 tablespoons of the fat to the pan.

Raise the heat to medium, add the onion to the pan, and cook, stirring often, until softened but not browned, about 5 minutes. Add the garlic and cook, stirring, just until fragrant, about 30 seconds. Add the coffee, maple syrup, sugar, and vinegar, stir well, and bring to a simmer. Reduce the heat to low and simmer gently, stirring occasionally, until thickened, about 20 minutes. Add the bacon and continue to cook, stirring often, until syrupy, about 5 minutes longer.

Let the mixture cool, then transfer to a food processor and pulse to a slightly chunky spread. Season with salt and pepper. (The jam can be made up to 1 week in advance and stored in an airtight container in the refrigerator.)

To make the crostini, preheat the oven to 350°F. Brush a large sheet pan with oil and arrange the baguette slices in a single layer on the prepared pan. Brush the tops of the slices with oil and season with salt and pepper. Bake until crisp and golden, 15–18 minutes. (The crostini can be baked up to 1 day in advance, cooled, and stored in an airtight container at room temperature.)

To assemble, spread each crostino with some of the bacon jam and top with a wedge of the cheese. Arrange on a large platter and serve.

WINE COUNTRY COCKTAIL PARTY

Pomegranate Gin Fizz

At its simplest, a gin fizz is a cocktail made with gin, egg white, lemon, sugar, and club soda. In keeping with the season, we use a pomegranate-blueberry juice blend with a splash of orange liqueur. Don't be put off by the raw egg white. Shaking it vigorously with the other ingredients will give the drink a frothy richness that is well worth the effort.

MAKES 4 COCKTAILS

8 oz JCB Gin or other gin

16 oz pomegranate-blueberry juice

2 oz orange liqueur, such as Grand Marnier

1 large egg white (about 1 oz)

Ice cubes, for shaking and serving

About 8 oz club soda, chilled

4 lime wedges

Combine the gin, pomegranate-blueberry juice, liqueur, and egg white in a cocktail shaker. Fill with ice and shake vigorously for 2 minutes.

Strain into 4 highball glasses over ice cubes, dividing it evenly. Top with the club soda, garnish with a lime wedge, and serve.

WINE COUNTRY COCKTAIL PARTY

Passion Fruit–Blood Orange Kiss

This sparkling wine autumn sipper is easy to make, lower in alcohol than most cocktails, and pops with the flavors of the season. It's also incredibly pretty. You'll find blood oranges in farmers' markets and in the produce aisle of supermarkets in the fall and winter months. Look for passion fruit juice in bottles and aseptic cartons at well-stocked supermarkets.

MAKES 4 COCKTAILS

4 oz fresh blood orange juice, chilled

2 oz store-bought passion fruit juice, chilled

¾ oz Campari

1 bottle (750 ml) Champagne or sparkling wine, such as JCB French Kiss, chilled

4 thin blood orange slices, for garnish

Put 4 champagne flutes in the freezer at least 15 minutes before serving.

Combine the orange juice, passion fruit juice, and Campari in a stirring glass or small pitcher and stir well. Remove the flutes from the freezer and divide the mixture evenly among them. Top with the Champagne. Garnish with the orange slices and serve.

Note: Oakville Grocery proprietor Jean-Charles Boisset makes a sparkling rosé that is the perfect match for this cocktail—and with a name like French Kiss, how can you resist?

WINE COUNTRY COCKTAIL PARTY

Apple Bourbon Old-Fashioned

Apples grow plentifully in Northern California, so it's only natural that we are including a seasonal take on a classic of the mixologist's repertoire, the old-fashioned. Make the apple cider syrup well in advance so it has time to chill. Once you have it ready, watch your guests line up for this well-balanced beverage.

MAKES 4 COCKTAILS

3 cups apple cider

¼ cup firmly packed dark brown sugar

8 oz bourbon, such as Calistoga Depot Prosperous & Penniless Bourbon Whiskey

6 dashes of Angostura bitters

1 oz water

Ice cubes, for stirring and serving

8 very thin apple slices, for garnish

4 orange twists, for garnish

In a saucepan over medium-low heat, simmer the cider until it is reduced to ½ cup, about 20 minutes. Add the sugar and stir until dissolved. Pour the cider syrup into a small heatproof bowl and nest the bowl in an ice bath. Let cool completely. Transfer to an airtight container and refrigerate for at least 1 hour before using or up to 1 week.

Combine the bourbon, bitters, 2 oz (¼ cup) of the cider syrup, and the water in a stirring glass or cocktail shaker. Fill with ice and stir gently until well mixed.

Strain into 4 highball glasses over ice cubes, dividing it evenly. Garnish each cocktail with 2 apple slices and an orange twist and serve.

Note: The spirit of Oakville Grocery is alive and well at the Calistoga Depot, founded in 1868, where Boisset has created a Distillery honoring the history of Depot founder Sam Brannan. The Depot Distillery makes a small-batch bourbon whiskey finished in oak wine casks that have aged Buena Vista Napa Valley Cabernet Sauvignon.

LOCAL ARTISAN

EARTH & SKY CHOCOLATES

From bonbons to bars, the jewel-toned edible works of art at this Napa Valley–based chocolate boutique are the benchmark of balance and technical perfection.

It's often said, "they're too pretty to eat"! Anyone who has tried them knows they also live up to that beauty in both taste and texture.

Founded over a decade ago by chef Christian Parks, Earth & Sky Chocolates was created with the intent of producing artistic, European-quality confections in small batches using time-honored methods. From the beginning, the company strove to incorporate local ingredients, such as wildflower honey, lavender, rosemary, citrus, and locally distilled bourbon, to ensure the spirit of Napa Valley was present in every chocolate it made.

Today, Christian and proprietor Robbie Schmidt are committed to continuing age-old traditions by combining the finest-quality ingredients with the desire to leave a lasting impression on the palate. But they are also passionate about both contemporary innovation and leaving no chocolate lover behind, so they not only offer gluten-free confections but also an extensive selection of vegan bonbons. In the words of Robbie, the CCO (Chief Chocolatier Officer), "Simply put, I feel like Juliette Binoche in *Chocolat*. Bon appétit!"

PHOTOGRAPHS: LEFT: DYLAN ELLIOTT; RIGHT: EARTH & SKY CHOCOLATES

FALL PIZZA PARTY

Wild Mushroom, Caramelized Onion, and Goat Cheese Pizza

One of the most popular options on our wood-fired pizzas menu, this white pizza—meaning no red sauce—is made for all the mushroom lovers out there. At Oakville, we use a mixture of six types of mushrooms: white button, cremini, maitake, shiitake, king oyster (aka king trumpet), and oyster. Using different types delivers a variety of tastes and textures, so strive for a good mix using whatever mushrooms are available near you.

MAKES 1 PIZZA

One 8-oz ball pizza dough, homemade (page 205) or store-bought

1 tablespoon olive oil, plus more for brushing

¼ lb mixed wild and cultivated mushrooms, brushed clean, trimmed, and chopped

1 teaspoon finely chopped fresh thyme leaves

Kosher salt and freshly ground pepper

Semolina or fine cornmeal, for dusting

3 oz fresh goat cheese, such as Skyhill chèvre, crumbled

¼ cup Balsamic Caramelized Onions (page 208)

If using homemade dough, cover the dough ball and let come to room temperature for 4–6 hours; for store-bought dough, let the dough come to room temperature for 2–3 hours.

About 30 minutes before you are ready to bake the pizza, position a rack in the upper third of the oven, about 6 inches from the heat source, and place a pizza stone on the rack. Preheat the oven to 550°F (or as high as your oven will go). Once the oven comes to temperature, let the stone continue to heat for 15 minutes longer.

While the oven heats, cook the mushrooms. In a heavy frying pan, preferably cast iron, over medium-high heat, warm the oil. Add the mushrooms and thyme, season with salt and generously with pepper, and cook, stirring every so often, just until the mushrooms are lightly cooked, about 3 minutes. The timing will depend on the type and the size of the mushroom pieces. Remove from the heat. If there is liquid in the pan, drain the mushrooms.

When the oven and the stone are preheated, turn off the oven and turn on the broiler while you assemble the pizza. On a lightly floured work surface, gently pull the dough into a thin round crust about 10 inches in diameter. Dust a pizza peel with semolina and slide the dough onto the peel. (If you don't have a peel, use a rimless cookie sheet or an inverted sheet pan.) Distribute the cheese in an even layer on the dough. Top evenly with the mushrooms and then the onions.

Turn off the broiler and return the oven temperature to 550°F. Carefully slide the pizza onto the hot pizza stone and bake until the crust is golden brown and the top is bubbly, about 8 minutes. Using the peel, remove from the oven and transfer to a cutting board. Brush the edges of the dough with oil. Cut into wedges and serve.

FALL PIZZA PARTY

Mascarpone, Speck, and Arugula Pizza

Dollops of rich mascarpone cheese serve as the sauce for this pizza that layers creamy, salty, and peppery flavors. A specialty of northeastern Italy, speck is a lightly smoked, salt-cured ham. If unavailable, prosciutto, which has a milder flavor, can be substituted. Upgrade this pizza with a scattering of bite-size pieces of roasted winter squash, adding them with the mascarpone.

MAKES 1 PIZZA

One 8-oz ball pizza dough, homemade (page 205) or store-bought

Semolina or fine cornmeal, for dusting

¼ lb mascarpone cheese

Olive oil, for brushing

8 very thin slices speck, skin removed (about 1½ oz)

½ cup arugula

¼ cup grated Parmesan cheese

If using homemade dough, cover the dough ball and let come to room temperature for 4–6 hours; for store-bought dough, let the dough come to room temperature for 2–3 hours.

About 30 minutes before you are ready to bake the pizza, position a rack in the upper third of the oven, about 6 inches from the heat source, and place a pizza stone on the rack. Preheat the oven to 550°F (or as high as your oven will go). Once the oven comes to temperature, let the stone continue to heat for 15 minutes longer.

When the oven and the stone are preheated, turn off the oven and turn on the broiler while you assemble the pizza. On a lightly floured work surface, pull the dough into a thin round crust about 10 inches in diameter. Dust a pizza peel with semolina and slide the dough onto the peel. (If you don't have a peel, use a rimless cookie sheet or an inverted sheet pan.) Add the mascarpone in tablespoonfuls, arranging the clumps evenly over the dough.

Turn off the broiler and return the oven temperature to 550°F. Carefully slide the dough onto the hot pizza stone and bake until the crust is golden brown, about 8 minutes. Using the peel, remove from the oven and transfer to a cutting board. Immediately brush the edges of the dough with oil and spread the mascarpone into an even layer. Cut the pizza into 8 wedges. Lay a slice of speck on each wedge, then top the pizza evenly with the arugula and Parmesan and serve.

FALL PIZZA PARTY

Spicy Sausage, Tomato, and Fontina Pizza

We cook all of our pizzas to order in our outdoor wood-fired pizza oven, which means we are limited to sunny days. Fortunately, here in California wine country, we have a lot of those! This popular pizza combines spicy Mexican-style chorizo, creamy Fontina cheese, and two kinds of tomato to make a very special pie. If you like, add a sprinkle of dried oregano and some cooked potato slices to the mix.

MAKES 1 PIZZA

One 8-oz ball pizza dough, homemade (page 205) or store-bought

¼ lb spicy fresh Mexican-style chorizo, preferably Hobbs, casing removed (about 1 sausage link)

Semolina or fine cornmeal, for dusting

¼ cup puréed tomatoes

2 oz Fontina cheese, thinly sliced

¼ cup diced tomatoes, preferably heirloom

Olive oil, for brushing

If using homemade dough, cover the dough ball and let come to room temperature for 4–6 hours; for store-bought dough, let the dough come to room temperature for 2–3 hours.

About 30 minutes before you are ready to bake the pizza, position a rack in the upper third of the oven, about 6 inches from the heat source, and place a pizza stone on the rack. Preheat the oven to 550°F (or as high as your oven will go). Once the oven comes to temperature, let the stone continue to heat for 15 minutes longer.

While the oven heats, cook the chorizo. Warm a small cast-iron frying pan over medium-high heat. Crumble the chorizo into the pan and cook, breaking up the chorizo with the side of a wooden spoon, until browned and cooked through, about 8 minutes. Drain off any fat.

When the oven and the stone are preheated, turn off the oven and turn on the broiler while you assemble the pizza. On a lightly floured work surface, pull the dough into a thin round crust about 10 inches in diameter. Dust a pizza peel with semolina and slide the dough onto the peel. Spread the puréed tomatoes in an even layer over the dough. Top evenly with the chorizo, Fontina, and diced tomatoes.

Turn off the broiler and return the oven temperature to 550°F. Carefully slide the pizza onto the hot pizza stone and bake until the crust is golden brown and the top is bubbly, about 8 minutes. Using the peel, remove from the oven and transfer to a cutting board. Immediately brush the edges of the dough with oil. Cut into wedges and serve.

FALL PIZZA PARTY

Thai Crunch Mezzaluna

There's everything crunchy in this cabbage-kale salad studded with vegetables, fruits, and peanuts, which we dress with our potent dressing of sweet chili sauce and lime juice. We like tucking this vibrant salad into pizza crusts to make our popular mezzalunas, but you can also serve the salad as a side dish. Or you can add 1 cup shredded cooked chicken and/or 1 cup cooked rice vermicelli noodles for a main course.

MAKES 2 MEZZALUNAS

Two 8-oz balls pizza dough, homemade (page 205) or store-bought

Semolina or fine cornmeal, for dusting

Olive oil, for brushing

Kosher salt and freshly ground pepper

3 cups store-bought coleslaw mix

1 cup finely chopped kale

1 cup Sweet Chili Lime Dressing (page 215)

½ English cucumber, peeled and diced

1 small carrot, peeled and shredded

½ red bell pepper, seeded and diced

½ Granny Smith apple, halved, cored, and diced

½ cup drained and chopped canned mandarin segments

3 green onions, white and green parts, thinly sliced on the diagonal

¼ cup roasted peanuts

¼ cup chopped fresh cilantro

2 tablespoons chopped fresh mint

If using homemade dough, cover the dough balls and let come to room temperature for 4–6 hours; for store-bought dough, let the dough come to room temperature for 2–3 hours.

About 30 minutes before you are ready to bake the pizza crusts, position a rack in the upper third of the oven, about 6 inches from the heat source, and place a pizza stone on the rack. Preheat the oven to 550°F (or as high as your oven will go). Once the oven comes to temperature, let the stone continue to heat for 15 minutes longer.

When the oven and the stone are preheated, turn off the oven and turn on the broiler while you prep the dough. Working with 1 dough ball at a time, on a lightly floured work surface, pull the dough into a thin round crust about 8 inches in diameter. Dust a pizza peel with semolina and slide the dough onto the peel. (If you don't have a peel, use a rimless cookie sheet or an inverted sheet pan.) Brush the dough with oil and season with salt and pepper.

Turn off the broiler and return the oven temperature to 550°F. Carefully slide the crust onto the hot pizza stone and bake until golden brown, 6–8 minutes. Using the peel, remove from the oven and transfer to a cutting board. Repeat with the second dough ball.

To make the salad, in a large bowl, toss together the coleslaw mix and kale. Drizzle with ¼ cup of the dressing, then use your hands to massage the kale and cabbage slightly to soften it. Add the cucumber, carrot, bell pepper, apple, mandarin, green onions, peanuts, cilantro, and mint and toss gently to combine. Season with salt and pepper and add more dressing if you like.

Divide the salad between the pizza crusts. Fold one side of each crust over the salad, cut in half crosswise, and serve with the remaining dressing alongside.

FALL PIZZA PARTY

Yogurt Panna Cotta with Fresh Figs

Panna cotta, a soft, delicate, chilled Italian cream-based pudding, makes a light and refreshing end to a robust meal. Vanilla bean and orange zest flavor this yogurt-based version, giving it a heady fragrance. When figs are in season in early fall, they make a delightful accompaniment. If they are unavailable, select other fruit depending on the season, such as blackberries in summer, blood orange segments in winter, or poached rhubarb in spring.

MAKES 6 SERVINGS

2½ teaspoons (1 package) unflavored gelatin powder

1½ cups whole milk

1 vanilla bean, split lengthwise

½ cup sugar

3 orange zest strips, each 2-3 inches long

2 cups plain whole-milk yogurt

12 fresh figs, stems trimmed and quartered lengthwise

Honey, for drizzling

In a small bowl, sprinkle the gelatin over ½ cup of the milk. Let stand without stirring until the gelatin is moistened, about 10 minutes.

Pour the remaining 1 cup milk into a small saucepan. Scrape the seeds from the vanilla bean halves and add them to the milk and then add the pod. Add the sugar and orange zest strips, set the pan over medium heat, and bring to a simmer, stirring to dissolve the sugar. Remove from the heat.

Add the gelatin mixture to the milk mixture and stir until completely dissolved, about 3 minutes. Transfer to a large bowl and let cool until lukewarm, about 10 minutes. Remove the vanilla pod and zest strips. (The vanilla pod halves can be rinsed, dried, and buried in a small canister of sugar for vanilla sugar.) Whisk in the yogurt until well blended.

Divide the yogurt mixture among six ¾-cup ramekins or custard cups. Cover each with plastic wrap and refrigerate until set, at least 8 hours or up to 2 days.

To serve, run a thin knife blade around the inside edge of each ramekin to loosen the panna cotta, then invert onto a plate (or serve in the ramekins). Garnish with the figs and a drizzle of honey and serve.

FALL PIZZA PARTY

Bitter Greens Salad with Pear and Toasted Walnuts

This salad puts all the flavors of autumn in a bowl: bitter endive, peppery arugula, toasty walnuts, and crisp Asian pears. We toss this seasonal mix with a lemon vinaigrette, which lends a bright note and just the barest hint of sweetness.

MAKES 6 SERVINGS

3 Asian or Bosc pears, halved, cored, and cut into $1/8$-inch-thick slices

Juice of $1/2$ lemon

3 heads Belgian endive, cored and cut lengthwise into narrow strips

3 cups arugula

$1/2$ cup chopped walnuts, toasted

$1/2$ cup Lemon Vinaigrette (page 213)

Kosher salt and freshly ground pepper

In a large bowl, combine the pears and lemon juice and toss to coat evenly to prevent the pears from browning.

Add the endive, arugula, and walnuts to the pears. Drizzle with some of the vinaigrette, season with salt and pepper, and toss to coat evenly. Taste and add more vinaigrette, salt, and pepper if needed.

Divide the salad evenly among salad plates and serve.

MENUS
—

WINTER

Holiday Brunch Gathering

Afternoon Spritz Party

Winter Wine and Cheese Party

Wine Country Family Dinner

RECIPES

HOLIDAY BRUNCH GATHERING

Coconut–Chocolate Chip Overnight Oats 158

Egg, Ham, and Spinach Croissants 159

Egg, Bacon, and Cheddar Croissants 161

Sweet Potato Hash 162

Blood Orange–Pomegranate Mimosa 165

Hazelnut Streusel Bread 166

AFTERNOON SPRITZ PARTY

Bay Shrimp Rémoulade Sliders 167

Brie and Prosciutto Crostini with Fig Jam 171

Winter Greens Salad with Apples and Roasted Pecans 172

Oakville Chicken-Bacon Club Mezzaluna with Caesar Dressing 174

Meyer Lemon French 69 177

Sparkling Ginger Limeade 178

WINTER WINE AND CHEESE PARTY

Marinated Gremolata Olives 179

The Oakville Classic Charcuterie Board 180

Parmesan and Black Pepper Gougères 182

Broccoli-Almond Salad with Grapes and Bacon 183

Red and Gold Beet Salad with Pistachios and Feta 185

Tre Formaggi Pizza 188

Chicken and Gruyère Sandwiches with Bacon and Balsamic Onions 189

WINE COUNTRY FAMILY DINNER

Roasted Winter Root Vegetables with Herb Butter 192

Baked Butternut Squash Mac and Cheese 193

Brussels Sprouts, Arugula, and Dried Apricots Salad 195

Herbed Roast Chicken 196

Pear-Almond Custard Tart 199

Garlic Butter Dinner Rolls 201

HOLIDAY BRUNCH GATHERING

Coconut–Chocolate Chip Overnight Oats

Start your morning off right with overnight oats, which are easy to prep in advance and endlessly versatile. Our favorite version uses a blend of coconut milk, yogurt, and chia seeds that mingles with the rolled oats overnight. Serve the oats in cute jars—perfect for brunch—with bowls of toppings alongside for diners to add as they wish.

MAKES 4 SERVINGS

2 cups old-fashioned rolled oats

1⅓ cups coconut milk or milk of your choice

1 cup plain yogurt

4 tablespoons maple syrup, or to taste

4 teaspoons chia seeds (optional)

1 teaspoon pure vanilla extract

Kosher salt

2 cups fresh raspberries

½ cup chopped roasted almonds

½ cup unsweetened shredded dried coconut, toasted

¼ cup mini chocolate chips

Line up four 12-oz glass jars with lids on a work surface. To each jar, add ½ cup of the oats, ⅓ cup of the coconut milk, ¼ cup of the yogurt, 1 tablespoon of the maple syrup, 1 teaspoon of the chia seeds (if using), ¼ teaspoon of the vanilla, and a pinch of salt. Tightly cap each jar and shake well. Refrigerate for at least 4 hours or ideally overnight.

Spoon the overnight oats into individual bowls (or leave in the jars). Top each serving with the berries, almonds, coconut, and chocolate chips, dividing them evenly, and serve.

HOLIDAY BRUNCH GATHERING

Egg, Ham, and Spinach Croissants

Caramelized onions and a pinch of sweet baby spinach give these breakfast sandwiches color, texture, and memorable flavor. We like to use thin slices of Black Forest ham, but you can trade them out for prosciutto or crisp bacon, or leave out the meat completely for a tasty vegetarian option.

MAKES 2 SANDWICHES

3 large eggs

1 tablespoon milk

Kosher salt and freshly ground pepper

2 large croissants, split horizontally

2 large slices Cheddar cheese

2–3 oz thinly sliced Black Forest ham

1 tablespoon unsalted butter

¼ cup Balsamic Caramelized Onions (page 208)

¼ cup baby spinach

Preheat the oven to 350°F.

While the oven heats, in a bowl, whisk together the eggs and milk, then season with salt and pepper. Set aside.

Arrange the croissants on half of a sheet pan and the ham on the other half of the pan. Place in the oven until warmed, about 5 minutes.

Transfer each croissant to a plate. Turn the bottom halves cut side up and place a slice of Cheddar on each one, tearing the cheese to fit, then top the cheese with the ham, dividing it evenly.

In a nonstick frying pan over medium-low heat, melt the butter. When the butter is foamy, add the eggs and cook until set into a thin, flat omelet, about 2 minutes. Remove from the heat and divide the omelet in half.

Add a folded omelet half to each croissant, placing it on top of the ham. Then top the omelet with the onions and spinach, dividing them evenly. Cap with the croissant tops and serve.

Oakville Grocery | The Cookbook   159

HOLIDAY BRUNCH GATHERING

Egg, Bacon, and Cheddar Croissants

A holiday brunch deserves something special, and there's no more decadent breakfast sandwich than one served on a flaky, buttery croissant. Fry the bacon in advance, then warm the croissants, top with the cheese, and fry the eggs just before serving. No matter what time of year you serve these morning sandwiches, your gathering will feel like a holiday celebration.

MAKES 2 SANDWICHES

4 slices thick-cut bacon

2 large croissants, split

2 large slices Cheddar cheese

1 tablespoon olive oil

2 large eggs

Kosher salt and freshly ground pepper

Preheat the oven to 350°F.

While the oven heats, in a nonstick frying pan over medium-low heat, cook the bacon, turning once or twice, until the fat renders and the bacon becomes crispy, about 8 minutes. Transfer to paper towels to drain. Wipe out the pan.

Arrange the croissants on a sheet pan and place in the oven until warmed, about 5 minutes. Transfer each croissant to a plate. Turn the bottom halves cut side up and place a slice of Cheddar on each one, tearing the cheese to fit.

To make the eggs, in the frying pan over medium heat, warm the oil. Crack the eggs into the pan and season with salt and pepper. Cover the pan, reduce the heat to medium-low, and cook until the whites set, about 2 minutes for over easy eggs (or flip the eggs and cook to the desired consistency).

Place an egg on top of each Cheddar slice. Top each egg with 2 bacon slices. Cap with the croissant tops and serve.

HOLIDAY BRUNCH GATHERING

Sweet Potato Hash

This delicious vegetarian hash made with orange sweet potatoes, Yukon Gold potatoes, and an abundance of herbs and other vegetables is a riot of color and flavor. Top it with a couple of poached eggs and you have a complete meal, or serve it alongside egg-based breakfast sandwiches for a festive gathering. It's also pretty great with panfried sausages.

MAKES 6 SERVINGS

2 tablespoons olive oil, plus more for the pan

1½ lb orange-fleshed sweet potatoes, peeled and finely diced

1½ lb Yukon Gold potatoes, peeled and finely diced

1 yellow onion, finely chopped

1 red bell pepper, seeded and chopped

1 jalapeño chile, seeded and minced

1 cup fresh or thawed frozen corn kernels

1½ teaspoons ground cumin

3 tablespoons chopped fresh cilantro, plus more for garnish

Kosher salt and freshly ground pepper

Plain whole-milk yogurt, for serving

Lime wedges, for serving

Preheat the oven to 400°F. Lightly oil a large sheet pan. Pile the sweet potatoes and Yukon Gold potatoes on the prepared pan, drizzle with 1 tablespoon of the oil, and toss to coat evenly. Spread into an even layer and roast for 30 minutes. Using a metal spatula, turn the potatoes and continue roasting until lightly browned and tender, about 15 minutes longer. Remove from the oven and keep warm.

Meanwhile, in a large frying pan over medium heat, warm the remaining 1 tablespoon oil. Add the onion, bell pepper, and jalapeño and cook, stirring occasionally, until the vegetables are tender, about 10 minutes. Stir in the corn and cook, stirring often, until heated through, about 3 minutes. Stir in the cumin and cook, stirring, until fragrant, about 30 seconds. Add the potatoes and cilantro and stir to mix well. Season with salt and pepper.

Divide the hash among individual bowls. Top each serving with a dollop of yogurt and a sprinkle of cilantro, and serve with the lime wedges alongside.

HOLIDAY BRUNCH GATHERING

Blood Orange–Pomegranate Mimosa

No brunch is complete without a mimosa (at least that's how we feel). We add a touch of elegance to the familiar cocktail by using blood orange juice and pomegranate juice and then garnishing each glass with pomegranate seeds, an orange wheel, and a fresh mint sprig. Everyone is sure to want seconds.

MAKES 4 COCKTAILS

4 oz fresh blood orange juice

4 oz pomegranate juice

¾ oz Campari

1 bottle (750 ml) JCB Champagne or sparkling wine, chilled

For garnish

4 thin blood orange slices

A small handful of pomegranate seeds

4 fresh mint sprigs

Put 4 champagne flutes into the freezer at least 15 minutes before serving.

Combine the orange juice, pomegranate juice, and Campari in a stirring glass or small pitcher and stir well. Remove the flutes from the freezer and divide the mixture evenly among them. Top with the Champagne. Garnish with the orange slices, pomegranate seeds, and mint sprigs and serve.

HOLIDAY BRUNCH GATHERING

Hazelnut Streusel Bread

A thick slice of this hazelnut bread, which conceals a layer of streusel at its center, begs to be paired with a steaming cup of coffee or tea. It is wonderful brunch fare but also makes a satisfying afternoon snack or a lovely evening dessert. To make it dessert worthy, serve it with a scoop of vanilla ice cream and drizzles of dark chocolate sauce.

MAKES 1 LOAF

For the streusel

3 tablespoons all-purpose flour

¼ cup firmly packed light brown sugar

1 teaspoon ground cinnamon

3 tablespoons unsalted butter, melted

½ cup toasted and peeled hazelnuts, roughly chopped

For the batter

6 tablespoons unsalted butter, at room temperature, plus more for the pan

⅓ cup toasted and peeled whole hazelnuts

⅔ cup granulated sugar

1¼ cups all-purpose flour

2 teaspoons baking powder

½ teaspoon baking soda

Scant ½ teaspoon kosher salt

2 large eggs

1 teaspoon pure vanilla extract

¾ cup sour cream or plain whole-milk yogurt

½ cup mini semisweet chocolate chips or chunks (optional)

To make the streusel, in a food processor, combine the flour, brown sugar, cinnamon, and melted butter and process until crumbly. Transfer to a bowl and stir in the chopped hazelnuts. Set aside.

Preheat the oven to 350°F. Generously butter a 9 x 5-inch loaf pan.

To make the batter, in the food processor, process the whole hazelnuts and half of the granulated sugar until the nuts are finely ground. Add the flour, baking powder, baking soda, and salt and process to combine. Transfer to a large bowl.

In the food processor, process the room-temperature butter and the remaining granulated sugar until light and creamy, stopping and scraping down the sides of the bowl with a rubber spatula as needed. Add the eggs and vanilla and process until fully combined. Add the sour cream and process until incorporated. Scrape into the bowl with the flour mixture and stir together. Stir in the chocolate chips (if using).

Scrape about half of the batter into the prepared pan, spreading it evenly. Sprinkle about half of the streusel evenly over the top. Dollop the remaining batter over the streusel and spread it evenly in the pan. Top with the remaining streusel.

Bake the loaf until a toothpick inserted into the center comes out clean, about 50 minutes. Let cool in the pan on a wire rack for about 10 minutes, then remove from the pan and let cool completely on the rack. Cut into slices to serve.

AFTERNOON SPRITZ PARTY

Bay Shrimp Rémoulade Sliders

Tiny bay shrimp mix deliciously with piquant rémoulade, a French cousin of tartar sauce. We pile the shrimp salad on slider buns with pea shoots and pickled onions, which makes for easy party fare. This recipe yields a little more rémoulade than you need for the sliders, but the leftover sauce is great with grilled fish, crab cakes (page 131), or as a dipping sauce for fries.

MAKES 8–10 SLIDERS

For the rémoulade

½ cup mayonnaise, homemade (page 210) or store-bought

¼ cup sour cream

1 tablespoon Dijon mustard

1 tablespoon finely chopped cornichons

1 tablespoon capers, finely chopped

1 tablespoon finely chopped fresh flat-leaf parsley

1 tablespoon finely chopped fresh tarragon leaves

2 teaspoons white wine vinegar

2 teaspoons fresh lemon juice

1 teaspoon hot pepper sauce

½ teaspoon sweet paprika

¼ teaspoon sugar (optional)

Kosher salt and freshly ground pepper

1 lb cooked bay shrimp

8–10 slider buns, split

4 tablespoons unsalted butter, melted

1½ cups trimmed pea shoots

Pickled Onions (page 208)

To make the rémoulade, in a bowl, stir together the mayonnaise, sour cream, mustard, cornichons, capers, parsley, tarragon, vinegar, lemon juice, hot pepper sauce, paprika, and sugar (if using). Season with salt and pepper. Cover and refrigerate for at least 1 hour or up to overnight to allow the flavors to meld.

Rinse and dry the shrimp. Put the shrimp into a bowl and season with salt. Spoon half of the rémoulade over the shrimp and stir to combine. If you prefer a saucier shrimp rémoulade, add more rémoulade to achieve the consistency you like. Taste and season with salt and pepper and more lemon juice if needed. (The remaining rémoulade can be stored in an airtight container in the refrigerator for up to 1 week.)

Brush the cut side of each bun half lightly with the butter. In a large frying pan over medium heat, working in batches, toast the bun halves, cut side down, until golden brown. Transfer the bun halves, cut side up, to a platter.

Put a pinch of the pea shoots on the bottom of each bun and top with a scoop of the shrimp rémoulade. Top with the remaining pea shoots and the pickled onions, dividing them evenly. Cap with the bun tops and serve.

LOCAL ARTISAN

BAYVIEW PASTA

At his San Francisco-based Bayview Pasta, Sonoma County native Joshua Felciano has mastered the art of crafting delicious, small-batch pastas from his own fresh-milled flour.

He sources all his non-GMO whole grains from West Coast farms and takes pride in knowing exactly where and how they were grown and in buying them directly from the farmer, rather than an anonymous grain elevator.

Flour milled from whole grains has a short shelf life, so Joshua makes sure to turn it into pasta within a day or so and to get it out to stores and restaurants soon after. Every one of Bayview's handmade pastas, from its spaghettoni and rigatoni to its bucatini, fettuccine, and more, is marked with a milled date that reflects Joshua's passion for and commitment to quality at each step of the process.

Joshua has long been around pasta, as a restaurant chef for many years before opening Bayview Pasta and, before that, as a kid growing up in an Italian American family in Healdsburg. He knows his way around pizza, too, and if you're lucky, you will come across him selling his wood-fired pies from the back of his Piaggio Ape.

PHOTOGRAPHS: DOMINIC FELICIANO

AFTERNOON SPRITZ PARTY

Brie and Prosciutto Crostini with Fig Jam

Making crostini is a great way to use up a slightly stale baguette, and the crunchy toasts can be made up to a day in advance. That means that when it's party time, all you have to do is top the toasts and serve them with, perhaps, a glass of sparkling wine. Crostini toppings are limited only by your imagination. Here, prosciutto is topped with creamy Brie and a dollop of sticky fig jam—ingredients perfectly in tune with the season.

MAKES 8 SERVINGS

For the crostini

Extra-virgin olive oil, for brushing

1 baguette, cut crosswise into ¼-inch-thick slices

Salt and coarsely ground pepper

¼ lb very thinly sliced prosciutto

¾ lb good-quality Brie cheese

⅔ cup fig jam

To make the crostini, preheat the oven to 350°F. Brush a large sheet pan with oil and arrange the baguette slices in a single layer on the prepared pan. Brush the tops with oil and season with salt and pepper. Bake until crisp and golden, 15–18 minutes. (The crostini can be baked up to 1 day in advance, cooled, and stored in an airtight container at room temperature.)

To assemble, top each crostino with about ½ slice prosciutto, folding it to fit. Top the prosciutto with a slice of Brie and 1–2 teaspoons jam. Arrange on a large platter and serve.

AFTERNOON SPRITZ PARTY

Winter Greens Salad with Apples and Roasted Pecans

We love to draw inspiration for our menu from the local farmers' markets, where we can see what is growing nearby year-round. Although winter produce is not as bountiful as what's offered in other seasons, it is no less interesting. This salad balances the bitter greens of winter with a sweet-tangy vinaigrette, crunchy apples, and toasty pecans to create a lively, flavorful mix that both respects the time of year and will satisfy guests.

MAKES 4 SERVINGS

2 cups chopped watercress

2 cups chopped radicchio

2 cups chopped escarole

½ cup Golden Balsamic Vinaigrette (page 214)

Kosher salt and freshly ground pepper

1 large crisp, tart-sweet apple, such as Honeycrisp or Pink Lady, halved, cored, and thinly sliced

½ cup roughly chopped pecans, toasted

Parmesan cheese, for shaving

In a large serving bowl, combine the watercress, radicchio, and escarole. Drizzle with some of the vinaigrette, season with salt and pepper, and toss to coat lightly. Add the apple and pecans and toss to mix, adding more vinaigrette if needed. Using a vegetable peeler, shave the Parmesan over the salad, then serve, passing any remaining vinaigrette alongside.

AFTERNOON SPRITZ PARTY

Oakville Chicken-Bacon Club Mezzaluna with Caesar Dressing

We took the classic club sandwich and gave it an Oakville spin by turning the sandwich fillings into a salad and then sandwiching the salad in a folded pizza crust. *Mezzaluna* means "half-moon," which is the shape of the crust once you have folded it over the salad. Each mezzaluna will feed one really hungry person or two moderate eaters.

MAKES 2 MEZZALUNAS

Two 8-oz balls pizza dough, homemade (page 205) or store-bought

2 boneless, skinless chicken breast halves (8–12 oz total)

Kosher salt and freshly ground pepper

Olive oil, for rubbing and brushing

4 slices thick-cut bacon, cut into 1-inch pieces

Semolina or fine cornmeal, for dusting

6 heaping cups chopped romaine hearts

1 large heirloom tomato, chopped

⅓ cup shredded Parmesan cheese

1 cup Caesar Dressing (page 215)

If using homemade dough, cover the dough balls and let come to room temperature for 4–6 hours; for store-bought dough, let the dough come to room temperature for 2–3 hours.

Using a meat mallet, lightly pound each chicken breast to an even thickness of ¾–1 inch. Season the chicken all over with salt and pepper and rub with oil.

Prepare a fire in a charcoal or gas grill for direct cooking over medium heat (350°F–400°F). Brush the grill grate clean. Grill the chicken, with the lid closed, until it releases easily from the grate, about 4 minutes. Turn and grill the other side until opaque all the way through, about 4 minutes. Set aside to cool for at least 10 minutes. Chop the chicken into bite-size pieces.

About 30 minutes before you are ready to bake the pizza crusts, position a rack in the upper third of the oven, about 6 inches from the heat source, and place a pizza stone on the rack. Preheat the oven to 550°F (or as high as your oven will go). Once the oven comes to temperature, let the stone continue to heat for 15 minutes longer.

While the oven preheats, cook the bacon. In a frying pan over medium-low heat, cook the bacon, stirring once or twice, until the fat renders and the bacon becomes crispy, about 6 minutes. Using a slotted spoon, transfer to paper towels to drain.

(continued)

AFTERNOON SPRITZ PARTY

When the oven and the stone are preheated, turn off the oven and turn on the broiler while you prep the dough. Working with 1 dough ball at a time, on a lightly floured work surface, pull the dough into a thin round crust about 8 inches in diameter. Dust a pizza peel with semolina and slide the dough onto the peel. (If you don't have a peel, use a rimless cookie sheet or an inverted sheet pan.) Brush the dough with oil and season with salt and pepper.

Turn off the broiler and return the oven temperature to 550°F. Carefully slide the crust onto the hot pizza stone and bake until golden brown, 6–8 minutes. Using the peel, remove from the oven and transfer to a cutting board. Repeat with the second dough ball.

To assemble, in a large bowl, combine the romaine, chicken, bacon, tomato, and Parmesan. Drizzle with some of the dressing and toss gently to coat evenly. Season with salt and pepper and add more dressing if you like.

Divide the salad between the pizza crusts. Fold one side of each crust over the salad, cut in half crosswise, and serve with the remaining dressing alongside.

AFTERNOON SPRITZ PARTY

Meyer Lemon French 69

Meyer lemons are actually not even a lemon, but a cross between an orange and a lemon. They are excellent when you want the flavor of lemon but something a little milder, and they work particularly well in desserts and cocktails. You can adjust the sweetness of this classic lemon cocktail by adding more or less simple syrup.

MAKES 4 COCKTAILS

6 oz JCB Gin or other gin

2 oz fresh lemon juice

2 oz Simple Syrup (page 215)

Ice cubes, for shaking

8 oz JCB No. 69 Brut Rosé or sparkling wine, chilled

4 Meyer lemon twists, for garnish

Put 4 champagne flutes into the freezer at least 15 minutes before serving.

Combine the gin, lemon juice, and simple syrup in a cocktail shaker. Fill with ice, cover, and shake vigorously for 10 seconds until thoroughly chilled.

Double strain among the chilled flutes, dividing it evenly, then top with JCB No. 69 Brut Rosé. Garnish with the lemon twists and serve.

AFTERNOON SPRITZ PARTY

Sparkling Ginger Limeade

Limes—and all citrus—are plentiful throughout California, especially in the winter months, their prime season. So we are always looking for delicious ways to make use of that bounty. To make this drink into lemonade, simply switch out the lime juice for an equal amount of lemon juice—or try half lemon and half lime.

MAKES 6 SERVINGS

4 cups tap water

2/3 cup sugar

1/2 cup peeled and sliced fresh ginger

3/4 cup fresh lime juice

Ice cubes, for serving

About 2 1/2 cups sparkling water, chilled

Lime slices, for garnish

In a saucepan, combine the tap water, sugar, and ginger and bring to a boil over medium-high heat, stirring to dissolve the sugar. Remove from the heat, cover, and set aside for 10 minutes.

Strain the ginger mixture through a fine-mesh sieve into a large glass jar or pitcher. Add the lime juice, stir well, cover, and refrigerate until well chilled, at least 1 hour or up to overnight.

Fill 6 tall glasses with ice. Divide the lime-ginger mixture evenly among the glasses and top off with the sparkling water. Gently stir each serving, then garnish with the lime slices and serve.

WINTER WINE AND CHEESE PARTY

Marinated Gremolata Olives

This recipe is based on the amazing olives from Bayview Pasta that we sell in the store. The best way to marinate these olives is to use the jar they came in: drain the olives, mix them with the aromatics, pack them back into the jar, and top them off with olive oil. If you buy the olives in bulk, use a pint jar with a lid. The marinated olives are easy to store and easy to transport, plus they go beautifully with any charcuterie board (page 180) or cheese plate (page 41).

MAKES 2 CUPS

1 jar (10 oz) Castelvetrano olives

1 clove garlic, minced

1 teaspoon minced fresh oregano leaves

1 teaspoon finely grated orange zest

1 teaspoon finely grated lemon zest

¼ teaspoon ground cumin

1 cup extra-virgin olive oil

Drain the olives into a fine-mesh sieve held over the sink; reserve the jar. In a bowl, mix together the olives, garlic, oregano, orange zest, lemon zest, and cumin. Pack the seasoned olives back into the jar and add the oil. Make sure the olives are submerged in the oil, adding more if needed, then cap the jar and shake to mix well.

Refrigerate for at least 1 day before serving. The olives can be stored in the jar in the refrigerator for up to 1 week.

WINTER WINE AND CHEESE PARTY

The Oakville Classic Charcuterie Board

No matter what kind of board we are making, we always aim for bounty and variety. For our charcuterie board, we like to use a mix of salamis, cured hams, and spreadable meats like 'nduja, pâté, or rillettes. But meats need accompaniments, so we surround them with dried and fresh fruits, nuts, and mustard and/or chutney. We also always include a bowl of olives, and our favorites come from Bayview Pasta. Make sure to include a variety of crackers, crostini, or baguette slices, too.

MAKES 6–8 SERVINGS

½ lb Italian salami, preferably Journeyman, thinly sliced

½ lb soppressata, preferably Journeyman, thinly sliced

½ lb prosciutto or serrano ham, sliced paper-thin

6 oz 'nduja (spreadable pork sausage; preferably Journeyman) country-style pâté (page 38), chicken liver mousse, or rillettes

3 oz dried Turkish apricots, sliced, or other dried fruit

About ⅔ cup (2 oz) salted roasted Marcona almonds or candied walnuts or pecans

Assorted crackers, crostini (page 171), or baguette slices

1 large bunch green or red grapes, divided into 3 or 4 clusters

About 1 cup Castelvetrano olives

Grainy mustard and/or fruit chutney

Arrange the salami, soppressata, prosciutto, and 'nduja on 1 or 2 large cutting boards or platters. Arrange the apricots, almonds, crackers, and grapes around the meats. Put the olives into a small bowl and add to the board with a smaller bowl alongside for pits. Spoon the mustard and/or chutney into small bowls, add to the board, and serve.

WINTER WINE AND CHEESE PARTY

Parmesan and Black Pepper Gougères

These bite-size cheese puffs go particularly well with a glass of light red wine, making them a natural addition to our wine and cheese party menu. Plus, despite being delicate pastries, they are quite easy to make. If you like, slightly underbake them, let cool, freeze them in a single layer, bag them, and store in the freezer. Then when unexpected guests arrive, just pop some in the oven for about 15 minutes and serve as a warm welcome.

MAKES ABOUT 24 GOUGÈRES

6 tablespoons unsalted butter, cut into pieces

½ cup whole milk

½ cup water

½ teaspoon kosher salt

½ teaspoon freshly ground pepper

1 cup all-purpose flour

4 large eggs

¾ cup grated Parmesan cheese

Preheat the oven to 425°F. Line two rimmed baking sheets with parchment paper.

In a saucepan over medium-high heat, melt the butter. Add the milk, water, salt, and pepper and bring to a rolling boil. Remove from the heat and quickly add the flour all at once. Beat vigorously with a wooden spoon until thoroughly blended, then return the pan to medium-high heat and beat until the mixture pulls away from the sides of the pan and comes together in a smooth, shiny ball, about 2 minutes.

Transfer the mixture to the bowl of a stand mixer fitted with the paddle attachment. Beat on low speed until it cools down slightly, 1–2 minutes. In a small bowl, lightly beat 1 of the eggs and add to the flour mixture. Beat on medium speed until the egg is completely incorporated and the mixture goes from shiny to matte. Repeat to add each of the remaining eggs, one at a time, beating well after each addition until the mixture is smooth. Add ½ cup of the Parmesan and beat until well mixed.

To shape the gougères, spoon the paste into a pastry bag fitted with a plain round tip ½ inch in diameter. Alternatively, spoon the paste into a resealable plastic bag, seal it closed, and snip off one bottom corner. Pipe mounds about 1 inch in diameter and ½ inch high onto the prepared pans, spacing the mounds 2 inches apart.

Sprinkle the remaining Parmesan evenly over the tops of the gougères, then press down gently so the Parmesan adheres. Be careful not to flatten the mounds. Bake, without opening the oven, until the gougères are lightly browned and nearly doubled in size, about 20 minutes. Transfer to wire racks to cool.

Serve warm or at room temperature. Leftover gougères will keep in an airtight container in the refrigerator for up to 1 week. Recrisp in a 350°F oven before serving.

WINTER WINE AND CHEESE PARTY

Broccoli-Almond Salad with Grapes and Bacon

Anyone who has tried this salad out of our deli case knows how uncommonly delicious and well-balanced it is. We like broccoli, but on its own it can be pretty boring. Add toasted almonds, salty bacon, and sweet grapes, dress everything with a creamy-sweet-tart dressing, and magic happens.

MAKES 4–6 SERVINGS

½ cup slivered blanched almonds

4 slices thick-cut bacon, chopped

1 lb broccoli florets and tender stems, cut into ½-inch pieces

½ lb red seedless grapes, halved

¼ red onion, diced

For the dressing

½ cup mayonnaise, homemade (page 210) or store-bought

1 tablespoon golden balsamic vinegar

2 teaspoons firmly packed light brown sugar

Pinch of kosher salt

In a frying pan over medium-low heat, toast the almonds, stirring often, until golden, about 3 minutes. Transfer two-thirds of the almonds to a large bowl and put the remaining almonds in a small bowl.

In the same pan over medium-low heat, cook the bacon, stirring once or twice, until the fat renders and the bacon becomes crispy, about 6 minutes. Using a slotted spoon, transfer to paper towels to drain.

Add the broccoli, grapes, onion, and bacon to the large bowl with the almonds.

To make the dressing, in a small bowl, whisk together the mayonnaise, vinegar, sugar, and salt. Taste and adjust the seasoning with more vinegar, sugar, and salt if needed.

Drizzle the dressing over the broccoli mixture and toss to coat evenly. Serve right away or cover and refrigerate for up to 1 day. Serve chilled or at room temperature.

WINTER WINE AND CHEESE PARTY

Red and Gold Beet Salad with Pistachios and Feta

Choose as many varieties of beets as you can find for a truly spectacular, colorful salad. We typically use a mixture of red beets and golden beets, but when we can also find pretty Chioggia (striped) beets, we throw them in as well. Make sure you roast the golden or striped beets separately from the red beets, which will color them red. (Red beets make a great natural Easter egg dye!)

MAKES 4–6 SERVINGS

2 large red beets, trimmed and halved

2 large golden beets, trimmed and halved

1 cup water

Kosher salt and freshly ground pepper

½ cup Golden Balsamic Vinaigrette (page 214)

½ cup crumbled feta cheese (about 2 oz)

¼ cup roasted pistachios

Preheat the oven to 400°F.

Put the red beets and golden beets in separate baking dishes just large enough to hold them. Add ½ cup of the water to each dish. Season the beets with salt and pepper. Cover each dish tightly with aluminum foil. Roast until tender when pierced with a knife, about 1 hour.

Let the beets cool in the baking dishes until warm, then remove and discard the skins. Cut all the beets into ¾-inch pieces and combine them in a shallow serving bowl.

Drizzle the beets with some of the vinaigrette. Top with the feta and pistachios and serve, passing additional vinaigrette alongside.

WINTER WINE AND CHEESE PARTY

Tre Formaggi Pizza

Our three-cheese pizza is a hit with old and young alike—making it an excellent addition to any family gathering. A simple combination of tomato sauce with Parmesan, mozzarella, and Fontina creates a springboard to other creative toppings. Turn it into a pizza quattro formaggi with the addition of crumbled blue cheese, or omit the tomato sauce and add caramelized onions (page 208) and sautéed greens or black olives.

MAKES 1 PIZZA

One 8-oz ball pizza dough, homemade (page 205) or store-bought

Semolina or fine cornmeal, for dusting

¼ cup puréed tomatoes

¼ cup grated Parmesan cheese

½ cup shredded whole-milk mozzarella cheese

¼ cup shredded Fontina cheese

Olive oil, for brushing

If using homemade dough, cover the dough ball and let come to room temperature for 4–6 hours; for store-bought dough, let the dough come to room temperature for 2–3 hours.

About 30 minutes before you are ready to bake the pizza, position a rack in the upper third of the oven, about 6 inches from the heat source, and place a pizza stone on the rack. Preheat the oven to 550°F (or as high as your oven will go). Once the oven comes to temperature, let the stone continue to heat for 15 minutes longer.

When the oven and the stone are preheated, turn off the oven and turn on the broiler while you assemble the pizza. On a lightly floured work surface, pull the dough into a thin round crust about 10 inches in diameter. Dust a pizza peel with semolina and slide the dough onto the peel. (If you don't have a peel, use a rimless cookie sheet or an inverted sheet pan.) Spread the tomatoes in an even layer over the dough. Top evenly with the Parmesan, then the mozzarella, and finally the Fontina.

Turn off the broiler and return the oven temperature to 550°F. Carefully slide the pizza onto the hot pizza stone and bake until the crust is golden brown and the cheese is bubbly, 6–8 minutes. Using the peel, remove from the oven and transfer to a cutting board. Immediately brush the edges of the dough with oil. Cut into wedges and serve.

WINTER WINE AND CHEESE PARTY

Chicken and Gruyère Sandwiches with Bacon and Balsamic Onions

This sandwich is delicious served at room temperature, but we think it becomes something special when you grill it in a panini press. If you don't have a panini press, grill the sandwiches in a cast-iron pan, preferably with a weight on top. For a party, slice the rolls crosswise into four or five pieces so guests can pile them on their plates with other small bites.

MAKES 2 SANDWICHES

2 boneless, skinless chicken breast halves

Kosher salt and freshly ground pepper

Olive oil, for rubbing

4 slices thick-cut bacon

¼ cup mayonnaise, homemade (page 210) or store-bought

1 tablespoon Dijon mustard

2 torpedo or hoagie rolls, split

¼ cup Balsamic Caramelized Onions (page 208)

¼ lb Gruyère cheese, thinly sliced

Using a meat mallet, lightly pound each chicken breast to an even thickness of ¾–1 inch. Season the chicken all over with salt and pepper and rub with oil. Set aside while you ready the grill.

Prepare a fire in a charcoal or gas grill for direct cooking over medium heat (350°F–400°F). Brush the grill grate clean. Grill the chicken, with the lid closed, until it releases easily from the grate, about 4 minutes. Turn and grill the other side until opaque all the way through, about 4 minutes. Set aside to cool for at least 10 minutes.

Meanwhile, in a frying pan over medium-low heat, cook the bacon, turning once or twice, until the fat renders and the bacon becomes crispy, about 8 minutes. Transfer to paper towels to drain. In a small bowl, stir together the mayonnaise and Dijon mustard.

Lay the roll halves, cut side up, on a work surface. Spread with the mayonnaise mixture, dividing it evenly. Top each roll bottom with a chicken breast, half of the caramelized onions, 2 slices bacon, and half of the Gruyère slices. Cap with the roll tops.

To grill the sandwiches, preheat an electric panini press on medium-low according to the manufacturer's instructions. Place the sandwiches, one at a time, on the preheated press and cook according to the manufacturer's instructions until the sandwich is warmed through and the cheese is melted, 6–8 minutes. Alternatively, heat a stove-top grill pan or heavy frying pan over medium heat. Add a sandwich and cook, pressing down firmly with a heavy lid and turning once, until the cheese melts, about 3 minutes on each side.

Transfer the sandwiches to a cutting board, cut in half, and serve.

LOCAL ARTISAN

JOURNEYMAN MEAT CO.

When he was only three years old, Peter Seghesio's father began teaching him how to cure *salumi* and make sausages.

The crafting of artisanal meat products was a tradition that went back generations in the Seghesio family, who emigrated from Italy to Sonoma County in the late 1800s.

Peter's grandparents were farmers and winemakers and established Seghesio Family Vineyards, which Peter took over in 1987. After two decades leading the family winery, Peter decided to take a new journey, drawing on his childhood memories of crafting Italian *salumi*.

Apprenticeships with famed butchers in Tuscany, Italy, guided Peter's newfound business, one that is built on the art of Italian whole-animal butchery and employs the same care used in wine production: slow aging, the absence of fillers common to mass-produced *salumi*, and a reliance on seasonal ingredients from local farms.

In a 2018 issue of *The Wine Industry Advisor*, Peter explained how his approach to *salumi* production parallels winemaking: "At Journeyman Meat Co. we apply the same approach to artisanal meat as we do winemaking. We source our own meats, make everything on site and know where everything is from."

PHOTOGRAPHS: JOURNEYMAN MEAT CO.

WINE COUNTRY FAMILY DINNER

Roasted Winter Root Vegetables with Herb Butter

What better way to showcase winter's vegetables than roasting them and tossing them with a fragrant herb butter. This is a great side dish to the roast chicken that anchors this menu, but it also nicely complements pan-seared steaks or even an old-fashioned pot roast.

MAKES 6 SERVINGS

½ lb carrots, peeled and cut into 1-inch pieces

½ lb parsnips, peeled and cut into 1-inch pieces

½ lb rutabagas, peeled and cut into 1-inch pieces

½ lb yams or sweet potatoes, peeled and cut into 1-inch pieces

2 tablespoons unsalted butter

1 tablespoon extra-virgin olive oil

2 teaspoons chopped fresh thyme leaves

2 teaspoons chopped fresh sage leaves

Kosher salt and freshly ground pepper

Preheat the oven to 450°F.

Bring a large pot three-fourths full of salted water to a boil over high heat. Add the carrots, parsnips, and rutabagas and simmer until the vegetables give slightly when pierced with a fork, about 4 minutes. Drain well. Transfer to a large sheet pan and add the yams.

In a small saucepan over low heat, melt the butter. Add the oil, thyme, and sage and stir to combine. Drizzle the butter-herb mixture over the vegetables and toss to coat evenly. Season with salt and pepper.

Roast, stirring occasionally, until the vegetables can be easily pierced with a knife tip, about 30 minutes. Transfer to a serving bowl and serve.

WINE COUNTRY FAMILY DINNER

Baked Butternut Squash Mac and Cheese

Whether offered as a side dish as in this menu or served as the main event, a big pan of homemade mac and cheese is always met with oohs and aahs. We've added diced roasted butternut squash to the dish, which you should take as an invitation to experiment with other additions, such as different types of winter squash, blanched broccoli, or sautéed mushrooms.

MAKES 6–8 SERVINGS

2 cups peeled and diced butternut squash

Olive oil, for drizzling

Kosher salt and freshly ground pepper

4 tablespoons unsalted butter, plus more for the baking dish

½ yellow onion, finely chopped

½ cup all-purpose flour

4 cups whole milk, warmed

2 cups shredded sharp white Cheddar cheese

1 lb dried macaroni

1 cup panko bread crumbs (optional)

Preheat the oven to 450°F.

Pile the squash on a sheet pan. Drizzle with oil, season with salt and pepper, and toss to coat evenly, then spread in an even layer. Bake, stirring once or twice, until browned and tender, about 10 minutes. Set aside while you make the mac and cheese.

Reduce the oven heat to 375°F. Butter a shallow 2-quart baking dish.

In a large saucepan over medium heat, melt the butter. Add the onion and cook, stirring, until tender, about 6 minutes. Sprinkle with the flour and cook, stirring constantly with a whisk or wooden spoon, until the flour and butter thicken into a paste and smell fragrant, about 1 minute. Do not let the roux brown. Slowly whisk in the milk until the sauce is hot, smooth, and blended. Add the cheese by the handful, stirring after each addition until it melts. Season with salt and pepper and remove from the heat.

Bring a large pot three-fourths full of water to a boil over high heat. Add 1 tablespoon salt and the macaroni and cook, stirring occasionally, according to the package instructions until al dente. Drain well.

Add the macaroni to the pan with the sauce and stir to coat evenly. Add the reserved butternut squash and stir gently to mix well. Transfer the mixture to the prepared dish, spreading it evenly. Sprinkle the panko over the top, if using.

Bake, uncovered, until lightly browned and bubbling, 35–40 minutes. Remove from the oven and serve.

WINE COUNTRY FAMILY DINNER

Brussels Sprouts, Arugula, and Dried Apricot Salad

Shaving raw Brussels sprouts gives them an entirely different flavor and texture, like a milder version of crisp cabbage. It's best to use a mandoline, but if you don't have one, a sharp chef's knife will work. The addition of apricots and currants adds a hint of sweetness, the nuts give the salad crunch, and the lemon vinaigrette imparts a bright note.

MAKES 6 SERVINGS

1 lb Brussels sprouts, trimmed

3 cups arugula

½ cup slivered blanched almonds, toasted

½ cup chopped dried apricots

¼ cup dried currants

½ cup Lemon Vinaigrette (page 213)

Kosher salt and freshly ground pepper

Using a mandoline, thinly shave the Brussels sprouts lengthwise. Alternatively, use a chef's knife to slice the sprouts lengthwise as thinly as possible. Transfer to a serving bowl.

Add the arugula and half each of the almonds, apricots, and currants to the bowl. Drizzle with some of the vinaigrette and toss to coat evenly. Season with salt and pepper. Garnish with the remaining almonds, apricots, and currants and serve with the remaining dressing alongside.

WINE COUNTRY FAMILY DINNER

Herbed Roast Chicken

There's something quite special, and celebratory, about a whole roasted chicken, and—thankfully—it is not at all difficult to make. In fact, we would go so far as to suggest that this recipe should be on weekly rotation. Our herb-infused chicken makes a great centerpiece for a family dinner, and leftovers are terrific in salads and sandwiches or stirred into soups.

MAKES 6 SERVINGS

2 teaspoons chopped fresh rosemary, plus one 4-inch sprig

1 tablespoon chopped fresh thyme, plus 3 sprigs

2 teaspoons chopped fresh sage, plus 1 sprig

¼ cup extra-virgin olive oil, plus more for rubbing

Kosher salt and freshly ground pepper

1 organic roasting chicken, about 5 lb

½ small yellow onion, halved

3 large cloves garlic, smashed

Preheat the oven to 425°F.

In a small bowl, stir together the chopped rosemary, thyme, and sage with the ¼ cup oil and season with pepper. Working from the neck end, gently separate the chicken skin from the meat with your fingers, being careful not to tear the skin. Rotate the bird 180 degrees and loosen the skin above the cavity the same way, reaching in as far as possible to loosen it on the tops of the thighs and legs. Slip the herb mixture between the skin and flesh and rub it evenly over the exposed meat, covering as much of it as possible. Pat the skin back into place and tuck the wing tips under.

Season the cavity with 2 teaspoons salt, then stuff it with the rosemary, thyme, and sage sprigs and the onion and garlic, pushing them in as far as they will go. Tie the legs together with kitchen string. (The chicken can be prepared up to this point a day in advance, wrapped well, and refrigerated.)

Rub the entire outside of the chicken with oil and season well with salt. Place the bird, breast side up, in a cast-iron pan just large enough to hold it. Roast until the juices run clear when a thigh is pierced, about 1 hour and 10 minutes (12–15 minutes per lb), or until an instant-read thermometer inserted in the thickest part of the thigh (not touching bone) registers 165°F. Let rest for 15 minutes before carving.

WINE COUNTRY FAMILY DINNER

Pear-Almond Custard Tart

This tart is worth making simply for the appealing fragrance that will fill your home while you poach the pears. The tender pears are then bathed in brandy-spiked custard and topped with toasted almonds and a crunchy sprinkle of sugar. Serve the wedges plain or dress them up with crème anglaise or softly whipped cream (to which you could add a splash of brandy).

MAKES 8 SERVINGS

For the poached pears

3 cups water

¾ cup sugar

3 ripe but firm pears, preferably Bosc, peeled, quartered, and cored

Peel of 1 orange, removed in strips with a vegetable peeler

½ vanilla bean, split lengthwise

Tart Dough (page 207)

1 large egg

¼ cup plus 1 tablespoon sugar

3 tablespoons all-purpose flour

½ cup heavy cream

1 teaspoon pure vanilla extract, or 2 tablespoons brandy (optional)

Pinch of kosher salt

¼ cup sliced almonds, lightly toasted

To poach the pears, cut a circle of parchment paper to fit the diameter of a medium saucepan. Fold the circle in half, cut a small half circle from the center, and then flatten the parchment again. In the saucepan, combine the water and sugar and bring to a boil over high heat, stirring to dissolve the sugar. Reduce the heat to medium and add the pears and orange peel. Scrape the seeds from the vanilla bean halves and add them to the pan along with the pod. Lay the parchment on top of the liquid in the saucepan to keep the pears submerged. Adjust the heat so the liquid simmers gently and poach the pears until just tender when pierced with a knife tip, 10–15 minutes. Remove from the heat and let the pears cool completely in the poaching liquid.

Preheat the oven to 400°F.

On a lightly floured work surface, roll out the dough into a 13-inch round about ⅛ inch thick. Carefully roll the dough around the rolling pin and position the pin over a 9½- or 10-inch tart pan with a removable bottom. Unroll the dough, centering it in the pan, then press gently onto the bottom and up the sides. Trim away any excess dough from the rim. Line the tart crust with parchment paper and fill with pie weights or dried beans.

Bake the tart crust until it is dry and is just starting to color a bit, about 20 minutes. (Check to see if the crust is ready by lifting up a corner of the paper.) Remove from the oven, remove the parchment and weights, and let the crust cool completely on a wire rack. Reduce the oven temperature to 350°F.

(continued)

Oakville Grocery | The Cookbook   199

WINE COUNTRY FAMILY DINNER

Pear-Almond Custard Tart (continued)

Cut each pear quarter lengthwise into 4 slices, then lay most of the pear slices in the crust in an overlapping circle close to the rim. Use the remaining slices to fill the middle.

In a bowl, beat together the egg and ¼ cup of the sugar until thick and pale. Beat in the flour and then the cream, vanilla (if using), and salt. Pour the custard evenly over the pears.

Bake the tart until the custard starts to puff up, about 10 minutes. Sprinkle the almonds and the remaining 1 tablespoon sugar evenly over the top of the tart and continue baking until the custard is set and lightly browned, 15–20 minutes longer. Let cool in the pan on a wire rack. The tart can be served warm or at room temperature. Just before serving, press the pan bottom up through the pan ring and, using an offset spatula, ease the tart from the pan bottom onto a serving plate. Cut into wedges to serve.

WINE COUNTRY FAMILY DINNER

Garlic Butter Dinner Rolls

These pillowy, buttery rolls deserve a place at every family gathering. The dough is brushed with garlic-parsley butter before and after baking, imparting lots of flavor. If garlic isn't your thing, you can leave it out and brush the rolls with parsley butter. These rolls are easy to transport, making them a welcome contribution to nearly any potluck.

MAKES 18 ROLLS

6 tablespoons unsalted butter, plus 4 tablespoons, melted and cooled

2 tablespoons sugar

1 cup whole milk

1 package (2¼ teaspoons) instant yeast

3 cups all-purpose flour

1 large egg, lightly beaten

2 teaspoons kosher salt

1 teaspoon garlic powder

1 teaspoon dried parsley

In a small saucepan over low heat, melt the 6 tablespoons butter with the sugar. Remove from the heat and stir in the milk (the mixture should not be more than 115°F). Pour into the bowl of a stand mixer. Whisk in the yeast and let stand until foamy, about 10 minutes.

Stir in the flour, egg, and salt. Attach the dough hook and knead the dough on medium speed for about 5 minutes. The dough will be soft and slightly sticky. Form the dough into a ball in the bowl, cover the bowl with plastic wrap, and let rise in a warm, draft-free spot until doubled in size, about 1 hour.

Butter the bottom and sides of a 9 x 13-inch baking pan with 1 tablespoon of the melted butter. Scrape the dough onto a floured work surface. Divide the dough into 18 equal pieces (each about 1½ oz). Roll each piece into a ball and place the balls in the prepared pan, spacing them evenly.

In a small bowl, stir together the remaining 3 tablespoons melted butter, the garlic powder, and parsley. Brush the dough balls generously with half of the butter mixture. Cover the pan loosely with plastic wrap and let stand in a warm, draft-free spot until the dough balls are puffy, about 1 hour. About 15 minutes before they are ready, preheat the oven to 375°F.

Bake the rolls until golden, about 18 minutes. Remove from the oven and immediately brush the rolls with the remaining butter mixture. Serve warm.

PANTRY STAPLES

Pizza Dough

Mimmo Russo, pizza captain of Oakville Grocery, hails from Naples, Italy, where he grew up on a farm. His mother told him that to make the best food, you first have to add *amore*, "that's the first ingredient, the love is inside." Mimmo, who has worked at Oakville Grocery since 2018, makes all the pizzas and pizza dough at the store, and you can often find him manning the wood-fired oven on the patio. He says that for the best Neapolitan-style pizza with dough that is soft and pillowy, you must do two things: use your hands to stretch the dough and be careful not to stretch it too thin "or you will end up with crackers!"

MAKES EIGHT 8-OZ DOUGH BALLS

For the "mother" dough

1 envelope (2¼ teaspoons) instant yeast

1½ cups lukewarm water (95°F to 100°F)

4½ cups "00" flour, preferably Caputo brand

For the final dough

1⅔ cups water

1½ tablespoons fine sea salt

4½ cups "00" flour, preferably Caputo brand, plus more as needed

Extra-virgin olive oil, for rubbing

Start the "mother" dough 4 days before you want to make the final pizza. So, for example, if you want pizza on Saturday evening, make the "mother" on Wednesday morning and let it sit at room temperature for 8–12 hours. On Wednesday evening, mix the final dough, put it in the refrigerator, and let it rise overnight. On Thursday morning, divide the dough into balls and shape them. Return the dough to the refrigerator for 2 days. On Saturday, pull out the dough about 4-6 hours before you want to make the pizzas. It sounds like a lot of time, but each step is quick and easy. The dough can be frozen, so you can make it in advance and then just thaw it at room temperature for 6–8 hours.

To make the "mother" dough, in a large bowl, sprinkle the yeast into the water and stir to combine. Add the flour and mix with your hands until well blended. Cover the bowl and set aside at room temperature for 8–12 hours.

To make the final dough, in the bowl of a stand mixer fitted with the dough hook, combine the water and salt and stir to dissolve the salt. Add the flour and mix on low speed until combined. Using wet hands, scrape the "mother" dough into the mixture. Knead on low speed until combined, about 1 minute, then set aside for 10 minutes to rest.

Knead the dough on low speed until a shaggy mass forms. Increase the speed to medium and knead until well mixed and the dough has softened, about 10 minutes. The dough should be soft and a little sticky. If it is overly wet, add a bit more flour. Scrape the dough down into a ball. Cover the bowl with plastic wrap and refrigerate overnight.

(continued)

PANTRY STAPLES

Line a large airtight container or sheet pan with parchment paper and lightly rub the parchment with oil. Turn the dough out onto a lightly floured work surface and divide it into 8 equal pieces (each about 8 oz). Shape each piece into a smooth ball, dusting with flour only if the dough becomes sticky. Arrange the dough balls on the parchment, spacing them apart, and rub them lightly with oil. Cover with a lid or plastic wrap. Refrigerate for 48 hours.

When you are ready to use the dough, pull out the number of dough balls you want to use and let sit, covered, at room temperature for 4–6 hours. The remaining dough can be individually wrapped in plastic wrap and frozen in a resealable freezer bag for up to 2 months. (When ready to use, thaw the frozen dough for 6–8 hours at room temperature.)

Gluten-Free Pizza Dough

MAKES FOUR 10-OZ DOUGH BALLS

2 cups lukewarm water (105°F–115°F), plus more as needed

2 tablespoons extra-virgin olive oil, plus more for the bowl and pan

1 package (2¼ teaspoons) instant yeast

1 teaspoon sugar

5¼ cups "00" gluten-free flour blend, preferably Caputo brand

1½ tablespoons fine sea salt

Extra-virgin olive oil, for the bowl and the pan

White rice flour, for dusting

In the bowl of a stand mixer, whisk together the water, oil, yeast, and sugar. Set aside until foamy, about 10 minutes.

Add the flour to the yeast mixture. Fit the mixer with the paddle attachment and beat on low speed until mixed, about 2 minutes. Add the salt and continue to beat on medium speed until well mixed, about 2 minutes. Reduce the speed to low and mix for 2 minutes. The dough will be thick and sticky. Oil a large bowl, transfer the dough to the bowl, cover, and refrigerate for at least 1 hour or up to 3 hours.

About 30 minutes before you are ready to bake, remove the dough from the refrigerator. Divide the dough into 4 equal pieces (each about 10 oz). (At this point, the dough can be wrapped in plastic wrap and frozen in a resealable freezer bag for up to 2 months. When ready to use, thaw the frozen dough for 3–4 hours at room temperature.)

Preheat the oven to 450°F. Lightly grease a sheet pan with oil. Lightly dust a work surface with rice flour. Roll out a dough ball into an 11-inch round. Transfer to the prepared pan and let rest for 15 minutes. To bake partially, bake the crust, flipping it over halfway through, just until set, about 9 minutes total. (To bake completely, such as for a mezzaluna, bake, flipping it over halfway through, until golden brown, 18–20 minutes total.) Top the crust with toppings, then return to the oven and bake until golden brown, about 10 minutes longer.

Alternatively, place a pizza stone in the oven and preheat the oven to 550°F. Lightly dust a work surface with rice flour. Roll out a dough ball into an 11-inch round. Slide the dough onto a peel and let rest for 15 minutes. (If you don't have a peel, use a rimless cookie sheet or an inverted sheet pan.) To bake partially, bake the crust, flipping it over halfway through, just until set, about 4 minutes. (To bake completely, such as for a mezzaluna, bake, turning once more, until golden brown, about 9 minutes total.) Top the crust with toppings, then return to the oven and bake until the crust is golden brown, about 5 minutes longer.

PANTRY STAPLES

Tart Dough

MAKES ENOUGH FOR ONE 9½- OR 10-INCH TART CRUST OR SIX 4½-INCH TARTLET SHELLS

1¼ cups all-purpose flour

¼ cup sugar

¼ teaspoon kosher salt

½ cup cold unsalted butter, cut into cubes

1 large egg yolk

2 tablespoons very cold water

1 teaspoon pure vanilla extract

In a food processor, combine the flour, sugar, and salt and pulse briefly to mix. Scatter the butter over the top and pulse until the mixture becomes crumbly and resembles coarse cornmeal, with butter pieces no larger than small peas. In a small bowl, whisk together the egg yolk, water, and vanilla. Add the egg mixture to the processor and pulse just until the dough is no longer dry and begins to clump together.

Transfer the dough to a work surface, shape into a ball, and then press into a thick disk. (At this point, the dough can be tightly wrapped and refrigerated for up to 1 day or frozen for up to 1 month. If frozen, thaw overnight in the refrigerator before using.)

For a 9½- or 10-inch tart: On a lightly floured work surface, roll out the dough into a 13-inch round about ⅛ inch thick. Carefully roll the dough around the rolling pin and position the pin over a 9½- or 10-inch tart pan with a removable bottom. Unroll the dough, centering it in the pan, then press gently onto the bottom and up the sides. Trim away any excess dough from the rim.

For 4½-inch tartlets: Divide the dough into 6 equal pieces. On a lightly floured work surface, roll out each piece into a round about ⅛ inch thick. Press each round into the bottom and up the sides of a 4½-inch tartlet pan and trim away any excess dough from the rim.

To bake the tart or tartlet shells fully, preheat the oven to 400°F. Prick the bottom of the tart or the tartlet shells with a fork. Freeze for 15 minutes.

Place the tartlet pans on a sheet pan. Line the tart or tartlet crusts with parchment paper and fill with pie weights or dried beans. Bake until dry and lightly golden, about 20 minutes. (Check if the crust is ready by lifting up a corner of the parchment.) Remove the foil and weights and continue to bake until golden brown, about 7 minutes longer. Let cool completely on a wire rack before filling.

Preserved Meyer Lemons

MAKES 6 PRESERVED LEMONS

1 cup kosher salt
6 Meyer lemons, well scrubbed and quartered through the stem end

1 cup fresh Meyer lemon juice, plus more as needed

Put the salt into a shallow bowl. One at a time, turn the lemon quarters in the salt, coating well, and place in a 1-quart canning jar. You may need to apply some gentle force to get the last few quarters into the jar. Add the salt remaining in the bowl and the lemon juice to the jar. If air bubbles are visible, cover the jar and shake it a little to eliminate them. Uncover the jar, add additional lemon juice to reach the lip of the jar, and then re-cover.

Store the jar on your countertop for 1 day. Uncover the jar and add more lemon juice if needed to cover the lemons completely, then cover again. Store on your countertop for 6 more days, shaking the jar once or twice a day. The lemons are now ready to use. They will keep in the refrigerator for up to 3 months.

PANTRY STAPLES

Caramelized Onions

MAKES ABOUT 1 CUP

2 tablespoons olive oil, or 1 tablespoon olive oil plus 1 tablespoon unsalted butter

3 large yellow onions, thinly sliced

Kosher salt

In a large frying pan over medium heat, warm the oil. Add the onions and cook, stirring every so often, until they start to soften, about 10 minutes. Reduce the heat to medium-low, sprinkle the onions with a little salt, and continue to cook, stirring occasionally, until the onions are richly browned, 30–45 minutes. If the onions start to get too dark, reduce the heat to low, and if they dry out too much, add a little water.

The onions can be used warm or at room temperature. They will keep in an airtight container in the refrigerator for up to 1 week.

Balsamic Caramelized Onions

MAKES ABOUT 1 CUP

1 tablespoon olive oil

2 large yellow onions, halved lengthwise and thinly sliced crosswise

2 tablespoons balsamic vinegar

1 tablespoon firmly packed light brown sugar

Kosher salt

In a large frying pan over medium-low heat, warm the oil. Add the onions and cook, stirring every so often, until they soften and start to brown, about 10 minutes. Reduce the heat to low, sprinkle the onions with the vinegar, sugar, and a pinch or two of salt, and continue to cook, stirring occasionally, until the onions are richly browned, about 30 minutes. Add a little water if the onions dry out too much.

The onions can be used warm or at room temperature. They will keep in an airtight container in the refrigerator for up to 1 week.

Pickled Onions

MAKES ABOUT 1 CUP

1 red onion, thinly sliced

Boiling water, for blanching

¼ cup rice vinegar

1 teaspoon sugar

½ teaspoon peppercorns

½ teaspoon kosher salt

1 teaspoon chopped fresh dill

Put the onion slices into a fine-mesh sieve. Hold the sieve over the sink and pour a few cups of boiling water over the onion, then drain well.

In a saucepan over medium heat, stir together the vinegar, sugar, peppercorns, and salt. Bring to a boil, add the onion, return to a boil, and simmer for 1 minute. Remove from the heat and let cool completely.

Transfer the onion to a bowl and stir in the dill. Cover and refrigerate for at least 2 hours before using. The onions will keep in an airtight container in the refrigerator for up to 5 days; bring to room temperature before using.

PANTRY STAPLES

Black Olive Tapenade

MAKES ABOUT 1¼ CUPS

10 oz pitted Niçoise or Kalamata olives, drained if jarred (about 1 heaping cup)

¼ cup packed chopped jarred roasted red pepper, preferably piquillo

1 small clove garlic, minced

Finely grated zest of 1 lemon

3 tablespoons extra-virgin olive oil

1 tablespoon fresh lemon juice

⅛ teaspoon red pepper flakes (optional)

In a food processor, combine all the ingredients and process until the texture is to your liking, either a coarse or a smooth purée. Use right away, or store in an airtight container in the refrigerator for up to 2 weeks.

Bacon Jam

MAKES ABOUT 1 CUP

1 lb thick-cut bacon, finely chopped

1 yellow onion, finely chopped

2 cloves garlic, minced

½ cup brewed strong coffee

¼ cup pure maple syrup

¼ cup firmly packed light brown sugar

3 tablespoons cider vinegar

Kosher salt and freshly ground pepper

In a large, heavy frying pan over medium-low heat, cook the bacon, stirring occasionally, until the fat renders and the bacon begins to brown (but not crisp), stirring often, about 10 minutes. Using a slotted spoon, transfer to paper towels to drain. Pour the fat into a small heatproof bowl and return 3 tablespoons of fat to the pan.

Raise the heat to medium, add the onion to the pan, and cook, stirring often, until softened but not browned, about 5 minutes. Add the garlic and cook, stirring, just until fragrant, about 30 seconds. Add the coffee, maple syrup, sugar, and vinegar, stir well, and bring to a simmer. Reduce the heat to low and simmer gently, stirring occasionally, until thickened, about 20 minutes. Add the bacon and continue to cook until syrupy, about 5 minutes longer.

Let the mixture cool, then transfer to a food processor and pulse to a slightly chunky spread. Season to taste with salt and pepper. Use right away, or store in an airtight container in the refrigerator for up to 1 week.

Basil Pesto

MAKES ABOUT 1 CUP

1 clove garlic

¼ cup pine nuts, lightly toasted

2 cups packed fresh basil leaves

½ cup extra-virgin olive oil

½ cup grated Parmesan cheese

Kosher salt and freshly ground pepper

With a food processor running, drop the garlic through the feed tube and process until minced. Turn off the processor, add the pine nuts, and pulse a few times to chop. Add the basil and pulse a few times to chop coarsely. Then, with the processor running, add the oil through the feed tube in a slow, steady stream and process until a smooth, moderately thick paste forms, stopping to scrape down the sides of the bowl as needed.

Transfer the paste to a bowl and stir in the Parmesan. Season with salt and pepper. Use right away, or transfer to a jar, top with a thin film of oil, cap tightly, and store in the refrigerator for up to 1 week.

Oakville Grocery | The Cookbook

PANTRY STAPLES

Romesco Sauce

MAKES ABOUT 1 CUP

½ cup chopped jarred roasted red bell peppers

⅓ cup slivered blanched almonds, lightly toasted

1 small slice sourdough bread, crust removed

1–2 cloves garlic, chopped

2 tablespoons red wine vinegar

¼ teaspoon smoked paprika

¼ cup olive oil

Kosher salt and freshly ground pepper

In a blender, combine the peppers, almonds, bread, garlic, vinegar, and paprika and blend until fairly smooth. With the blender running, add the oil in a slow, steady stream and blend until the sauce is smooth and emulsified. Season with salt and pepper.

Use right away, or store in an airtight container in the refrigerator for up to 2 weeks or in the freezer for up to 2 months; thaw at room temperature before using.

Mayonnaise

MAKES ABOUT 1½ CUPS

1 large egg

1 tablespoon fresh lemon juice

1 teaspoon Dijon mustard

½ cup canola oil

½ cup extra-virgin olive oil

Kosher salt

Add the egg, lemon juice, and Dijon mustard to the bottom of an immersion blender cup or similar-size tall, narrow container. Add the canola oil on top and let settle for 1 minute. Using an immersion blender, and starting at the bottom of the cup, turn on the blender and blend, tilting the blender to slowly emulsify the oil with the egg mixture. Transfer to a bowl. Slowly add the olive oil while whisking constantly. Season with salt.

Use right away, or store in an airtight container in the refrigerator for up to 1 week.

Balsamic Glaze

MAKES ABOUT ½ CUP

2 cups balsamic vinegar

In a small saucepan over medium-high heat, bring the vinegar to a boil. Reduce the heat to medium and simmer, stirring occasionally, until the vinegar becomes syrupy and reduces to about ½ cup, about 20 minutes. It should coat the back of a spoon.

Transfer to a heatproof jar and let cool completely. The glaze will thicken slightly as it cools. Use right away, or store in a tightly capped jar in the refrigerator for up to 2 weeks.

Chili Crisp Mayonnaise

MAKES ABOUT 1¼ CUPS

1 cup mayonnaise, homemade (above) or store-bought

¼ cup chili crisp

In a bowl, combine the mayonnaise and chili crisp and mix well. Taste and add more chili crisp if desired. Use right away, or store in an airtight container in the refrigerator for up to 1 week.

PANTRY STAPLES

Garlic Aioli

MAKES ABOUT 1 CUP

1 cup mayonnaise, homemade (page 210) or store-bought

1 small clove garlic, grated

1 teaspoon fresh lemon juice

In a bowl, combine all the ingredients and mix well. Use right away, or transfer to an airtight container and store in the refrigerator for up to 1 week.

Fresno Chile Aioli

MAKES ABOUT 1 CUP

2 teaspoons olive oil

4 Fresno chiles, seeded, if desired, and chopped

2 cloves garlic, grated

2 tablespoons cider vinegar

Pinch of kosher salt

1 cup mayonnaise, homemade (page 210) or store-bought

In a small frying pan over low heat, warm the oil. Add the chiles, garlic, vinegar, and salt and cook, stirring often, until the chiles are very tender, about 10 minutes. Let cool completely.

Transfer the cooled mixture to an immersion blender cup or similar-size tall, narrow container along with the mayonnaise and blend until puréed. (Alternatively, transfer to a mini blender or food processor and process until puréed.)

Use right away, or transfer to an airtight container and store in the refrigerator for up to 1 week.

Basil Aioli

MAKES ABOUT 1 CUP

1 cup mayonnaise, homemade (page 210) or store-bought

2 tablespoons finely chopped fresh basil leaves

1 small clove garlic, grated

1 teaspoon fresh lemon juice

In a bowl, combine all the ingredients and mix well. Use right away, or transfer to an airtight container and store in the refrigerator for up to 1 week.

Caper Aioli

MAKES ABOUT 1¼ CUPS

1 cup mayonnaise, homemade (page 210) or store-bought

1 tablespoon chopped capers

1 tablespoon finely chopped fresh basil leaves

1 tablespoon finely chopped fresh flat-leaf parsley leaves

1 small clove garlic, grated

1 tablespoon fresh lemon juice

In a bowl, combine all the ingredients and mix well. Use right away, or transfer to an airtight container and store in the refrigerator for up to 1 week.

Oakville Grocery | The Cookbook

PANTRY STAPLES

Lemon Aioli

MAKES ABOUT 1 CUP

1 cup mayonnaise, homemade (page 210) or store-bought

Finely grated zest of 1 lemon

2 tablespoons fresh lemon juice

1 clove garlic, minced

Kosher salt and freshly ground pepper

In a small bowl, combine the mayonnaise, lemon zest and juice, and garlic and mix well. Season with salt and pepper. Use right away, or transfer to an airtight container and store in the refrigerator for up to 1 week.

Preserved Meyer Lemon Aioli

MAKES ABOUT 1¼ CUPS

¼ preserved Meyer lemon (page 207)

1 cup mayonnaise, homemade (page 210) or store-bought

1 tablespoon fresh lemon juice

1 teaspoon minced fresh basil leaves

1 teaspoon minced fresh tarragon leaves

Remove and discard the flesh from the lemon quarter. Rinse the peel and then mince it and transfer to a small bowl. Add the mayonnaise, lemon juice, basil, and tarragon and mix well. Use right away, or transfer to an airtight container and store in the refrigerator for up to 1 week.

Chipotle Barbecue Sauce

MAKES ABOUT 2¼ CUPS

1 tablespoon canola oil

¼ cup chopped yellow onion

1 clove garlic, minced

1 can (7 oz) chipotle chiles in adobo sauce, drained, minced, and sauce reserved

1½ cups ketchup

¼ cup water

2 tablespoons firmly packed light brown sugar

1 tablespoon cider vinegar

1½ teaspoons Worcestershire sauce

¼ teaspoon freshly ground pepper

In a saucepan over medium heat, warm the oil. Add the onion and cook, stirring, until softened, about 5 minutes. Add the garlic and cook, stirring, until fragrant, about 30 seconds. Add the chipotle chiles and their sauce, ketchup, water, sugar, vinegar, Worcestershire sauce, and pepper and cook, stirring, until well mixed and the sauce has thickened, about 8 minutes.

If you prefer a smooth sauce, blend with an immersion blender until smooth. Use right away, or let cool completely, transfer to an airtight container, and store in the refrigerator for up to 2 weeks.

PANTRY STAPLES

Francisco's Tomato Salsa

MAKES ABOUT 2½ CUPS

2 lb Roma tomatoes (about 8 medium-large tomatoes)

½ large yellow onion, cut into ¼-inch-thick slices

3 large cloves garlic, unpeeled

1–3 small fresh chiles, such as Japones, Thai, árbol, jalapeño, or serrano

6 tablespoons extra-virgin olive oil

Kosher salt

2 tablespoons chopped chipotle chiles in adobo sauce, with sauce

1 tablespoon red wine vinegar

Position a rack in the upper third of the oven and preheat the oven to 450°F.

Core the tomatoes, halve lengthwise, and scoop out and discard the seeds. Arrange cut side down on a large sheet pan. Arrange the onion slices, garlic cloves, and fresh chiles (add according to taste) next to the tomatoes. Drizzle everything with 4 tablespoons of the olive oil, then season with salt.

Roast the vegetables until they are sizzling and the tomatoes are slightly charred and tender, about 20 minutes for the chiles and onion slices and about 30 minutes for the tomatoes and garlic. Keep an eye on the onion slices, chiles, and garlic and remove them as they become tender. If the tomatoes aren't charring, turn the oven to broil, return the pan to the oven, and char the tops.

When the vegetables are cool enough to handle, stem the chiles and then remove and discard the seeds if you like. Remove and discard the skins from the garlic cloves. Transfer the chiles and garlic to a blender. Add the tomatoes, onion slices, and any juices from the pan along with the chipotle chiles and their sauce and the vinegar. Blend on medium-high speed to a smooth purée. Taste and adjust the seasoning with vinegar and salt if needed.

Use right away, or transfer to an airtight container and store in the refrigerator for up to 2 weeks.

Lemon Vinaigrette

MAKES 1½ CUPS

½ cup fresh lemon juice

2 tablespoons rice vinegar

1 tablespoon honey

2 teaspoons Dijon mustard

½ teaspoon kosher salt

¼ teaspoon freshly ground pepper

½ cup extra-virgin olive oil

¼ cup canola oil

In a blender, combine the lemon juice, vinegar, honey, mustard, salt, and pepper and blend until well mixed. With the blender running, add both oils in a slow, steady stream and blend until the mixture is emulsified. Taste and adjust with more honey if needed.

Use right away, or transfer to an airtight jar and store in the refrigerator for up to 2 weeks. Bring to room temperature and shake well before using.

PANTRY STAPLES

Golden Balsamic Vinaigrette

MAKES ABOUT 1¼ CUPS

½ cup golden balsamic vinegar

1 tablespoon honey

2 teaspoons Dijon mustard

½ teaspoon kosher salt

¼ teaspoon freshly ground black pepper

½ cup extra-virgin olive oil

¼ cup canola oil

In a blender, combine the vinegar, honey, mustard, salt, and pepper and blend until well mixed. With the blender running, add both oils in a slow, steady stream and blend until the mixture is emulsified. Taste and adjust with more honey if needed.

Use right away, or transfer to an airtight jar and store in the refrigerator for up to 2 weeks. Bring to room temperature and shake well before using.

Greek Feta Vinaigrette

MAKES 1 CUP

¼ cup white wine vinegar

¼ cup crumbled feta cheese

2 tablespoons minced peperoncini

1 clove garlic, minced

1 teaspoon Dijon mustard

1 teaspoon honey

¼ cup extra-virgin olive oil

¼ cup canola oil

Kosher salt and freshly ground pepper

In a blender, combine the vinegar, feta, pepperoncini, garlic, mustard, honey, and both oils and blend until well mixed. Season with salt and pepper. Use right away, or transfer to an airtight jar and store in the refrigerator for up to 2 weeks. Bring to room temperature and shake well before using.

Tamari-Sesame Dressing

MAKES ABOUT 1 CUP

¼ cup reduced-sodium tamari

2 tablespoons toasted sesame oil

1 tablespoon balsamic vinegar

1 tablespoon honey

1½ teaspoons Dijon mustard

1½ teaspoons firmly packed light brown sugar

1 teaspoon Sriracha sauce

½ teaspoon ground mustard

⅛ teaspoon garlic powder

⅓ cup avocado or canola oil

In a blender, combine the tamari, sesame oil, vinegar, honey, Dijon mustard, sugar, Sriracha sauce, ground mustard, and garlic powder and blend until well mixed. With the blender running, add the avocado oil in a slow, steady stream and blend until the mixture is emulsified. Taste and adjust with more Sriracha sauce if needed. Use right away, or transfer to an airtight jar and store in the refrigerator for up to 2 weeks. Bring to room temperature and shake well before using.

PANTRY STAPLES

Caesar Dressing

MAKES ABOUT 1 CUP

1 large egg yolk

3 tablespoons fresh lemon juice

1 large clove garlic, minced

1–3 anchovy fillets in olive oil, finely chopped (optional)

2 teaspoons Dijon mustard

1 teaspoon Worcestershire sauce

1 teaspoon red wine vinegar

½ teaspoon kosher salt

Freshly ground pepper

¼ cup extra-virgin olive oil

¼ cup avocado or canola oil

In a blender, combine the egg yolk, lemon juice, garlic, anchovies to taste (if using), mustard, Worcestershire sauce, vinegar, salt, and a generous grinding of pepper and blend until smooth. With the blender running, add both oils in a slow, steady stream and blend until emulsified. Taste and adjust with lemon juice and salt if needed.

Use right away, or transfer to an airtight jar and store in the refrigerator for up to 4 days. Bring to room temperature and shake well before using.

Sweet Chili Lime Dressing

MAKES 1 CUP

½ cup sweet chili sauce

2 tablespoons reduced-sodium tamari

2 tablespoons fresh lime juice

1 tablespoon canola oil

1 tablespoon olive oil

2 teaspoons toasted sesame oil

½ teaspoon peeled and finely grated fresh ginger

Pinch of kosher salt

Pinch of freshly ground pepper

In a blender, combine all the ingredients and blend until well mixed. Use right away, or transfer to an airtight jar and store in the refrigerator for up to 2 weeks. Bring to room temperature and shake well before using.

Simple Syrup

MAKES ABOUT 1 CUP (375 ML)

1 cup (250 ml) water

1 cup (200 g) sugar

In a small saucepan over medium-high heat, bring the water to a simmer. Add the sugar and stir until the sugar is dissolved. Remove from the heat and let cool. Strain the syrup through a fine-mesh sieve into a clean container, cover, and refrigerate for up to 2 weeks.

Oakville Grocery | The Cookbook

Index

A

Aioli
- Basil Aioli, 211
- Caper Aioli, 211
- Fresno Chile Aioli, 211
- Garlic Aioli, 211
- Lemon Aioli, 212
- Preserved Meyer Lemon Aioli, 212

Almonds
- Blueberry-Almond Streusel Muffins, 26
- Broccoli-Almond Salad with Grapes and Bacon, 183
- Brussels Sprouts, Arugula, and Dried Apricots Salad, 195
- Coconut–Chocolate Chip Overnight Oats, 158
- The Oakville Classic Charcuterie Board, 180
- Oakville Signature Salad with Grilled Chicken, Blue Cheese, and Marcona Almonds, 123
- Pear-Almond Custard Tart, 199–200
- Romesco Sauce, 210

Apples
- Apple Bourbon Old-Fashioned, 140
- Apple Spice Hand Pies, 128
- Autumn Fruit Salad with Honey Vinaigrette, 112
- Crunchy Cabbage Slaw, 117
- Oakville Signature Salad with Grilled Chicken, Blue Cheese, and Marcona Almonds, 123
- Thai Crunch Mezzaluna, 155
- Winter Greens Salad with Apples and Roasted Pecans, 172

Apricots
- Brussels Sprouts, Arugula, and Dried Apricots Salad, 195
- California Cheese Plate with Stone Fruit Chutney, 41
- The Oakville Classic Charcuterie Board, 180

Artichokes
- Artichoke-Spinach Dip with Pita Chips, 49
- Cannellini Bean and Artichoke Salad, 124

Arugula
- Bitter Greens Salad with Pear and Toasted Walnuts, 152
- Brussels Sprouts, Arugula, and Dried Apricots Salad, 195
- Mascarpone, Speck, and Arugula Pizza, 146

Asparagus
- Asparagus Soup with Lemon and Chives, 31
- Hummus and Vegetable Crudités, 30
- Spring Green Salad, 34

Avocados
- Avocado Toast with Toasted Pepitas and Chili Crisp, 67
- BLTA Sandwiches, 81
- Curry Chicken Salad with Avocado, 100
- Kale Salad Mezzaluna with Golden Balsamic Dressing, 47
- Vegetable Wrap with Roasted Pepper Hummus, 50

B

Bacon
- Bacon Jam, 136, 206
- BLTA Sandwiches, 81
- BLT Deviled Eggs, 134
- Broccoli-Almond Salad with Grapes and Bacon, 183
- Chicken and Gruyère Sandwiches with Bacon and Balsamic Onions, 189
- Egg, Bacon, and Cheddar Croissants, 161
- Maple-Glazed Bacon, 68
- Oakville Chicken-Bacon Club Mezzaluna with Caesar Dressing, 174–75
- Rutherford Sandwiches, 20
- Turkey, Bacon, and Tomato Sandwiches, 106

Balsamic vinegar
- Balsamic Bloody Mary, 74
- Balsamic Caramelized Onions, 208
- Balsamic Glaze, 210
- Golden Balsamic Vinaigrette, 214

Barbecue Sauce, Chipotle, 212

Bars
- Summer Berry Streusel Bars, 107
- Triple Chocolate Brownies, 48

Basil
- Basil Aioli, 211
- Basil Pesto, 209
- Caprese Sandwiches with Balsamic Glaze, 80
- Summer Panzanella Salad, 103

Bayview Pasta, 168

BBQ Pulled Chicken Sandwiches with Slaw, 90

Beans
- Cannellini Bean and Artichoke Salad, 124
- Hummus, 30
- Hummus and Vegetable Crudités, 30
- from Rancho Gordo, 118

Beef
- Classic Oakville Burgers, 88
- Roast Beef Sandwiches with Olive Tapenade, 126
- Rocky's Reuben Sandwiches, 56
- Tri-Tip Sandwich Sliders, 133

Beer, from Mad Fritz Brewing Co., 96

Beet, Red and Gold, Salad with Pistachios and Feta, 185

Bellini, Peach, 84

Berries
- Blueberry-Almond Streusel Muffins, 26
- Coconut–Chocolate Chip Overnight Oats, 158
- Currant Cream Scones with Strawberry Jam, 70
- Strawberry Cream Tartlets, 59
- Summer Berry Streusel Bars, 107
- Summer Fruit Rosé Sangria, 57

Bloody Mary, Balsamic, 74

Blueberry-Almond Streusel Muffins, 26

Bourbon Apple Old-Fashioned, 140

Breads. See also Toasts
- Garlic Butter Dinner Rolls, 201
- Hazelnut Streusel Bread, 166
- Peach and Prosciutto Flatbread, 99
- Romesco and Skyhill Chèvre Flatbread, 129
- Summer Panzanella Salad, 103

Broccoli-Almond Salad with Grapes and Bacon, 183

Bromley, Derek, 28

Brownies, Triple Chocolate, 48

Brussels Sprouts, Arugula, and Dried Apricots Salad, 195

Burgers, Classic Oakville, 88

Burritos
- Chorizo and Potato Breakfast Burritos, 115
- Vegetable Breakfast Burritos, 116

C

Cabbage
  Crunchy Cabbage Slaw, 117
  Kale Salad Mezzaluna with Golden Balsamic Dressing, 47
  Slaw, 90
  Thai Crunch Mezzaluna, 150
Caesar Dressing, 15
Caper Aioli, 211
Caprese Sandwiches with Balsamic Glaze, 80
Carrots
  Crunchy Cabbage Slaw, 117
  Hummus and Vegetable Crudités, 30
  Roasted Winter Root Vegetables with Herb Butter, 192
  Sesame Noodle Salad, 39
  Thai Crunch Mezzaluna, 150
Ceviche, Hazel's Shrimp, 75
Charcuterie Board, The Oakville Classic, 180
Cheese
  Artichoke-Spinach Dip with Pita Chips, 49
  Baked Butternut Squash Mac and Cheese, 193
  Brie and Prosciutto Crostini with Fig Jam, 171
  California Cheese Plate with Stone Fruit Chutney, 41
  Caprese Sandwiches with Balsamic Glaze, 80
  Chicken and Gruyère Sandwiches with Bacon and Balsamic Onions, 189
  Classic Oakville Burgers, 88
  Egg, Bacon, and Cheddar Croissants, 161
  Egg, Ham, and Spinach Croissants, 159
  Greek Feta Vinaigrette, 214
  Grilled Corn, Tomato, and Roasted Pepper Salad with Cilantro, 93
  Mascarpone, Speck, and Arugula Pizza, 146
  Miyoko's Vegan Smoked Cheese Sandwiches, 33
  Mt Tam Cheese and Bacon Jam Crostini, 136
  Muffaletta Sandwiches, 125
  Oakville Signature Salad with Grilled Chicken, Blue Cheese, and Marcona Almonds, 123
  Parmesan and Black Pepper Gougères, 182
  Peach and Prosciutto Flatbread, 99
  Pesto Pasta Salad, 77
  from Point Reyes Farmstead Cheese Company, 42
  Quinoa Salad with Tomatoes and Feta, 36
  Red and Gold Beet Salad with Pistachios and Feta, 185
  Rocky's Reuben Sandwiches, 56
  Romesco and Skyhill Chèvre Flatbread, 129
  Rutherford Sandwiches, 20
  Smoked Salmon Sandwiches with Skyhill Chèvre, 53
  Spicy Sausage, Tomato, and Fontina Pizza, 147
  Tre Formaggi Pizza, 188
  Wagon Wheel and Rosemary Ham Sandwiches, 51
  Watermelon, Heirloom Tomato, Feta, and Mint Salad, 87
  Wild Mushroom, Caramelized Onion, and Goat Cheese Pizza, 145
  Yountville Sandwiches, 22
Cherries
  California Cheese Plate with Stone Fruit Chutney, 41
  Summer Fruit Rosé Sangria, 57
  Summer Fruit Smoothie, 69
Chicken
  BBQ Pulled Chicken Sandwiches with Slaw, 90
  Chicken and Gruyère Sandwiches with Bacon and Balsamic Onions, 189
  Curry Chicken Salad with Avocado, 100
  Francisco's Fried Chicken Tenders, 44
  Herbed Roast Chicken, 196
  Oakville Chicken-Bacon Club Mezzaluna with Caesar Dressing, 174–75
  Oakville Signature Salad with Grilled Chicken, Blue Cheese, and Marcona Almonds, 123
Chiles
  Chipotle Barbecue Sauce, 212
  Citrus-Chile Mignonette, 132
  Francisco's Tomato Salsa, 213
  Fresno Chile Aioli, 208
Chili crisp
  Avocado Toast with Toasted Pepitas and Chili Crisp, 67
  Chili Crisp Mayonnaise, 210
Chives
  BLT Deviled Eggs, 134
  Little Gem Salad with Herbed Green Goddess, 54
Chocolate
  Coconut-Chocolate Chip Overnight Oats, 158
  from Earth & Sky Chocolates, 142
  Triple Chocolate Brownies, 48
  Triple-Chocolate Chip Cookie Ice Cream Sandwiches, 95
Chutney, Stone Fruit, California Cheese Plate with, 41
Cilantro, Grilled Corn, Tomato, and Roasted Pepper Salad with, 93
Cinnamon-Sugar Muffins, Mini, 120
Citrus-Chile Mignonette, 132
Coconut
  Coconut-Chocolate Chip Overnight Oats, 158
  Maple-Coconut Granola and Yogurt Parfaits, 19
Coffee
  Cold Brew Iced Vanilla Latte, 27
  from Ohm Coffee Roasters, 28
Cookie, Triple-Chocolate Chip, Ice Cream Sandwiches, 95
Corn
  Grilled Corn, Tomato, and Roasted Pepper Salad with Cilantro, 93
  Sweet Potato Hash, 162
Crab Cakes, Bite-Size Dungeness, 131
Croissants
  Egg, Bacon, and Cheddar Croissants, 161
  Egg, Ham, and Spinach Croissants, 159
Crostini
  Brie and Prosciutto Crostini with Fig Jam, 171
  Mt Tam Cheese and Bacon Jam Crostini, 136
Cucumbers
  Cucumber-Lime Agua Fresca, 94
  Gazpacho, 104
  Hazel's Shrimp Ceviche, 75
  Hummus and Vegetable Crudités, 30
  Kale Salad Mezzaluna with Golden Balsamic Dressing, 47
  Quinoa Salad with Tomatoes and Feta, 36
  Summer Panzanella Salad, 103
  Thai Crunch Mezzaluna, 150
  Vegetable Romesco Sandwiches, 105
  Vegetable Wrap with Roasted Pepper Hummus, 50
  Watermelon, Heirloom Tomato, Feta, and Mint Salad, 87
Currant Cream Scones with Strawberry Jam, 70
Curry Chicken Salad with Avocado, 100

Oakville Grocery | The Cookbook **219**

D

Desserts
- Apple Spice Hand Pies, 128
- Hazelnut Streusel Bread, 166
- Pear-Almond Custard Tart, 199–200
- Strawberry Cream Tartlets, 59
- Summer Berry Streusel Bars, 107
- Triple Chocolate Brownies, 48
- Triple-Chocolate Chip Cookie Ice Cream Sandwiches, 95
- Yogurt Panna Cotta with Fresh Figs, 151

Dips
- Artichoke-Spinach Dip with Pita Chips, 49
- Hummus, 30

Dressings
- Caesar Dressing, 215
- Golden Balsamic Vinaigrette, 214
- Greek Feta Vinaigrette, 214
- Lemon Vinaigrette, 213
- Sweet Chili Lime Dressing, 215
- Tamari-Sesame Dressing, 214

Drinks
- Apple Bourbon Old-Fashioned, 140
- Balsamic Bloody Mary, 74
- Blood Orange–Pomegranate Mimosa, 165
- Cold Brew Iced Vanilla Latte, 27
- Cucumber-Lime Agua Fresca, 94
- Meyer Lemon French 69, 177
- Passion Fruit–Blood Orange Kiss, 139
- Peach Bellini, 84
- Pineapple-Mint Mocktail, 121
- Plant-Based Matcha Latte, 37
- Pomegranate Gin Fizz, 137
- Sparkling Ginger Limeade, 178
- Summer Fruit Rosé Sangria, 57
- Summer Fruit Smoothie, 69

E

Earth & Sky Chocolates, 142

Eggs
- BLT Deviled Eggs, 134
- Chorizo and Potato Breakfast Burritos, 115
- Deviled Eggs, 85
- Egg, Bacon, and Cheddar Croissants, 161
- Egg, Ham, and Spinach Croissants, 159
- Provençal Tuna Niçoise Sandwiches, 78
- Quinoa Breakfast Bowls with Potatoes, Spinach, and Pesto, 64
- Rutherford Sandwiches, 20
- Vegetable Breakfast Burritos, 116
- Yountville Sandwiches, 22

F

Fig Jam, Brie and Prosciutto Crostini with, 171
Figs, Fresh, Yogurt Panna Cotta with, 151

Fish
- Provençal Tuna Niçoise Sandwiches, 78
- Smoked Salmon Sandwiches with Skyhill Chèvre, 53

Fisher, Whitney, 96

Flatbreads
- Peach and Prosciutto Flatbread, 99
- Romesco and Skyhill Chèvre Flatbread, 129

French 69, Meyer Lemon, 177

Fruit. *See also* Berries; *specific fruits*
- Autumn Fruit Salad with Honey Vinaigrette, 112
- California Cheese Plate with Stone Fruit Chutney, 41
- Summer Fruit Rosé Sangria, 57
- Summer Fruit Smoothie, 69

G

Garlic Aioli, 211
Garlic Butter Dinner Rolls, 201
Gazpacho, 104

Gin
- Meyer Lemon French 69, 177
- Pomegranate Gin Fizz, 137

Ginger Limeade, Sparkling, 178
Glaze, Balsamic, 210
Gougères, Parmesan and Black Pepper, 182
Granola, Maple-Coconut, and Yogurt Parfaits, 19

Grapes
- Autumn Fruit Salad with Honey Vinaigrette, 112
- Broccoli-Almond Salad with Grapes and Bacon, 183
- The Oakville Classic Charcuterie Board, 180

Green Goddess, Herbed, Little Gem Salad with, 54

Greens. *See also specific greens*
- Bitter Greens Salad with Pear and Toasted Walnuts, 152
- Oakville Signature Salad with Grilled Chicken, Blue Cheese, and Marcona Almonds, 123
- Winter Greens Salad with Apples and Roasted Pecans, 172

H

Ham. *See also* Prosciutto
- Egg, Ham, and Spinach Croissants, 159
- Mascarpone, Speck, and Arugula Pizza, 146
- The Oakville Classic Charcuterie Board, 180
- Wagon Wheel and Rosemary Ham Sandwiches, 51
- Yountville Sandwiches, 22

Hand Pies, Apple Spice, 128
Hash, Sweet Potato, 162
Hazelnut Streusel Bread, 166

Herbs. *See also specific herbs*
- Little Gem Salad with Herbed Green Goddess, 54
- Rémoulade, 167

Hummus
- Hummus and Vegetable Crudités, 30
- Vegetable Wrap with Roasted Pepper Hummus, 50

I

Ice Cream Sandwiches, Triple-Chocolate Chip Cookie, 95

J

Jam
- Bacon Jam, 136, 209
- Strawberry Jam, 70
- Summer Berry Streusel Bars, 107

Journeyman Meat Co., 190

K

Kale
- Kale Salad Mezzaluna with Golden Balsamic Dressing, 47
- Thai Crunch Mezzaluna, 150

L

Latte
- Cold Brew Iced Vanilla Latte, 27
- Plant-Based Matcha Latte, 37

Lemons. *See also* Meyer lemons
- Lemon Aioli, 212
- Lemon Vinaigrette, 213

Lettuce
- BLTA Sandwiches, 81
- Little Gem Salad with Herbed

Green Goddess, 54
Oakville Chicken-Bacon
   Club Mezzaluna with
   Caesar Dressing, 174–75
Limeade, Sparkling Ginger, 178
Limes
   Cucumber-Lime Agua Fresca, 94
   Hazel's Shrimp Ceviche, 75
   Pineapple-Mint Mocktail, 121
   Sparkling Ginger Limeade, 178
   Sweet Chili Lime Dressing, 215

M

Mad Fritz Brewing Co., 96
Maple-Coconut Granola and
   Yogurt Parfaits, 19
Maple-Glazed Bacon, 68
Matcha Latte, Plant-Based, 37
Mayonnaise. *See also* Aioli
   Chili Crisp Mayonnaise, 210
   Mayonnaise, 210
Meyer lemons
   Meyer Lemon French 69, 177
   Preserved Meyer Lemon Aioli, 212
   Preserved Meyer Lemons, 207
Mezzaluna
   Kale Salad Mezzaluna with Golden
     Balsamic Dressing, 47
   Oakville Chicken-Bacon
     Club Mezzaluna with
     Caesar Dressing, 174–75
   Thai Crunch Mezzaluna, 150
Mignonette, Citrus-Chile, 132
Mimosa, Blood Orange–Pomegranate, 165
Mint
   Pineapple-Mint Mocktail, 121
   Watermelon, Heirloom Tomato, Feta,
     and Mint Salad, 87
Mitchell, Karen, 72
Mitchell Hansen, Sarah, 72
Model Bakery, 72
Muffaletta Sandwiches, 125
Muffins
   Blueberry-Almond Streusel Muffins, 26
   Mini Cinnamon-Sugar Muffins, 120
Mushrooms
   Vegetable Breakfast Burritos, 116
   Wild Mushroom, Caramelized Onion,
     and Goat Cheese Pizza, 145

N

Nectarines
   California Cheese Plate with Stone
     Fruit Chutney, 41

   Summer Fruit Rosé Sangria, 57
   Summer Fruit Smoothie, 69
Noodle Salad, Sesame, 39
Nuts. *See also specific nuts*
   Maple-Coconut Granola and Yogurt
     Parfaits, 19

O

Oats
   Coconut–Chocolate Chip
     Overnight Oats, 158
   Maple-Coconut Granola and
     Yogurt Parfaits, 19
   Summer Berry Streusel Bars, 107
Ohm Coffee Roasters, 28
Old-Fashioned, Apple Bourbon, 140
Olives
   Black Olive Tapenade, 209
   Marinated Gremolata Olives, 179
   Miyoko's Vegan Smoked Cheese
     Sandwiches, 33
   Muffaletta Sandwiches, 125
   The Oakville Classic Charcuterie
     Board, 180
   Provençal Tuna Niçoise Sandwiches, 78
   Quinoa Salad with Tomatoes
     and Feta, 36
   Roast Beef Sandwiches with
     Olive Tapenade, 126
Onions
   Balsamic Caramelized Onions, 208
   Bay Shrimp Rémoulade Sliders, 167
   Caramelized Onions, 208
   Chicken and Gruyère Sandwiches with
     Bacon and Balsamic Onions, 189
   Classic Oakville Burgers, 88
   Egg, Ham, and Spinach Croissants, 159
   Pickled Onions, 208
   Roasted Fingerling Potatoes with
     Peppers and Onions, 23
   Wild Mushroom, Caramelized Onion,
     and Goat Cheese Pizza, 145
Oranges
   Blood Orange–Pomegranate
     Mimosa, 165
   Passion Fruit–Blood
     Orange Kiss, 139
   Thai Crunch Mezzaluna, 150
Oysters with Citrus-Chile Mignonette, 132

P

Panna Cotta, Yogurt, with Fresh Figs, 151
Panzanella Salad, Summer, 103
Parfaits, Maple-Coconut Granola

   and Yogurt, 19
Parks, Christian, 142
Passion Fruit–Blood Orange Kiss, 139
Pasta
   Baked Butternut Squash Mac and
     Cheese, 193
   from Bayview Pasta, 168
   Pesto Pasta Salad, 77
Pastrami
   Rocky's Reuben Sandwiches, 56
Pâté Snack Board, French Country, 38
Peaches
   California Cheese Plate with Stone
     Fruit Chutney, 41
   Peach and Prosciutto Flatbread, 99
   Peach Bellini, 84
   Summer Fruit Rosé Sangria, 57
Pears
   Autumn Fruit Salad with Honey
     Vinaigrette, 112
   Bitter Greens Salad with Pear and
     Toasted Walnuts, 152
   Pear-Almond Custard Tart, 199–200
Peas and pea shoots
   Bay Shrimp Rémoulade Sliders, 167
   Spring Green Salad, 34
Pecans, Roasted, and Apples, Winter
   Greens Salad with, 172
Peppers. *See also* Chiles
   Gazpacho, 104
   Grilled Corn, Tomato, and Roasted
     Pepper Salad with Cilantro, 93
   Provençal Tuna Niçoise Sandwiches, 78
   Roasted Fingerling Potatoes with
     Peppers and Onions, 23
   Romesco Sauce, 210
   Sweet Potato Hash, 162
   Vegetable Romesco Sandwiches, 105
   Vegetable Wrap with Roasted Pepper
     Hummus, 50
Pesto
   Basil Pesto, 209
   Pesto Pasta Salad, 77
   Quinoa Breakfast Bowls with Potatoes,
     Spinach, and Pesto, 64
Pickled Onions, 208
Pies, Apple Spice Hand, 128
Pineapple-Mint Mocktail, 121
Pistachios and Feta, Red and Gold Beet
   Salad with, 185
Pita Chips, 49
Pizza and flatbreads
   Mascarpone, Speck, and
     Arugula Pizza, 146

Oakville Grocery | The Cookbook   **221**

Peach and Prosciutto Flatbread, 99
Romesco and Skyhill Chèvre
    Flatbread, 129
Spicy Sausage, Tomato, and Fontina
    Pizza, 147
Tre Formaggi Pizza, 188
Wild Mushroom, Caramelized Onion,
    and Goat Cheese Pizza, 145
Pizza Dough, 205-6
Pizza Dough, Gluten-Free, 206
Plums
    California Cheese Plate with Stone
        Fruit Chutney, 41
    Summer Fruit Smoothie, 69
Point Reyes Farmstead
    Cheese Company, 42
Pomegranate juice
    Blood Orange-Pomegranate Mimosa,
        165
    Pomegranate Gin Fizz, 137
Pork. See also Bacon; Ham; Sausage
    French Country Pâté Snack Board, 38
Potatoes
    Chorizo and Potato
        Breakfast Burritos, 115
    Oakville Potato Salad, 91
    Quinoa Breakfast Bowls with Potatoes,
        Spinach, and Pesto, 64
    Roasted Fingerling Potatoes with
        Peppers and Onions, 23
    Roasted Winter Root Vegetables
        with Herb Butter, 192
    Sweet Potato Hash, 162
    Vegetable Breakfast Burritos, 116
Preserved Meyer Lemon Aioli, 212
Preserved Meyer Lemons, 207
Prosciutto
    Brie and Prosciutto Crostini
        with Fig Jam, 171
    Muffaletta Sandwiches, 125
    The Oakville Classic Charcuterie
        Board, 180
    Peach and Prosciutto Flatbread, 99

Q

Quinoa Breakfast Bowls with Potatoes,
    Spinach, and Pesto, 64
Quinoa Salad with Tomatoes and Feta, 36

R

Radishes
    Hummus and Vegetable Crudités, 30
    Little Gem Salad with Herbed
        Green Goddess, 54

Spring Green Salad, 34
Rancho Gordo, 118
Raspberries
    Coconut-Chocolate Chip
        Overnight Oats, 158
    Summer Fruit Rosé Sangria, 57
Rémoulade, 167
Rolls, Garlic Butter Dinner, 201
Romesco
    Romesco and Skyhill Chèvre
        Flatbread, 129
    Romesco Sauce, 210
    Vegetable Romesco Sandwiches, 105

S

Salads
    Autumn Fruit Salad with
        Honey Vinaigrette, 112
    Bitter Greens Salad with Pear and
        Toasted Walnuts, 152
    Broccoli-Almond Salad with Grapes
        and Bacon, 183
    Brussels Sprouts, Arugula, and Dried
        Apricots Salad, 195
    Cannellini Bean and
        Artichoke Salad, 124
    Curry Chicken Salad with Avocado, 100
    Grilled Corn, Tomato, and Roasted
        Pepper Salad with Cilantro, 93
    Kale Salad Mezzaluna with Golden
        Balsamic Dressing, 47
    Little Gem Salad with Herbed Green
        Goddess, 54
    Oakville Potato Salad, 91
    Oakville Signature Salad with Grilled
        Chicken, Blue Cheese, and Marcona
        Almonds, 123
    Pesto Pasta Salad, 77
    Quinoa Salad with Tomatoes
        and Feta, 36
    Red and Gold Beet Salad with
        Pistachios and Feta, 185
    Sesame Noodle Salad, 39
    Spring Green Salad, 34
    Summer Panzanella Salad, 103
    Watermelon, Heirloom Tomato, Feta,
        and Mint Salad, 87
    Winter Greens Salad with Apples
        and Roasted Pecans, 172
Salami
    Muffaletta Sandwiches, 125
    The Oakville Classic
        Charcuterie Board, 180
Salmon, Smoked, Sandwiches with
    Skyhill Chèvre, 53

Salsa, Francisco's Tomato, 213
Sando, Steve, 118
Sandwiches
    BBQ Pulled Chicken Sandwiches with
        Slaw, 90
    BLTA Sandwiches, 81
    Caprese Sandwiches with Balsamic
        Glaze, 80
    Chicken and Gruyère Sandwiches with
        Bacon and Balsamic Onions, 189
    Egg, Bacon, and Cheddar Croissants,
        161
    Egg, Ham, and Spinach Croissants, 159
    Miyoko's Vegan Smoked Cheese
        Sandwiches, 33
    Muffaletta Sandwiches, 125
    Provençal Tuna Niçoise Sandwiches, 78
    Roast Beef Sandwiches with Olive
        Tapenade, 126
    Rocky's Reuben Sandwiches, 56
    Rutherford Sandwiches, 20
    Smoked Salmon Sandwiches with
        Skyhill Chèvre, 53
    Tri-Tip Sandwich Sliders, 133
    Turkey, Bacon, and Tomato
        Sandwiches, 106
    Vegetable Romesco Sandwiches, 105
    Wagon Wheel and Rosemary Ham
        Sandwiches, 51
    Yountville Sandwiches, 22
Sangria, Summer Fruit Rosé, 57
Sauces
    Chipotle Barbecue Sauce, 212
    Francisco's Tomato Salsa, 213
    Rémoulade, 167
    Romesco Sauce, 210
Sausage
    Chorizo and Potato Breakfast
        Burritos, 115
    from Journeyman Meat Co., 190
    Muffaletta Sandwiches, 125
    The Oakville Classic Charcuterie
        Board, 180
    Spicy Sausage, Tomato, and Fontina
        Pizza, 147
Schmidt, Robbie, 142
Scones, Currant Cream, with Strawberry
    Jam, 70
Seeds
    Avocado Toast with Toasted Pepitas and
        Chili Crisp, 67
    Maple-Coconut Granola and Yogurt
        Parfaits, 19
Seghesio, Peter, 190

Sesame
  Sesame Noodle Salad, 39
  Tamari-Sesame Dressing, 214
Shellfish
  Bay Shrimp Rémoulade Sliders, 167
  Bite-Size Dungeness Crab Cakes, 131
  Hazel's Shrimp Ceviche, 75
  Oysters with Citrus-Chile
    Mignonette, 132
Shrimp
  Bay Shrimp Rémoulade Sliders, 167
  Hazel's Shrimp Ceviche, 75
Slaw, BBQ Pulled Chicken
  Sandwiches with, 90
Slaw, Crunchy Cabbage, 117
Sliders
  Bay Shrimp Rémoulade Sliders, 167
  Tri-Tip Sandwich Sliders, 133
Smoked Salmon Sandwiches
  with Skyhill Chèvre, 53
Smoothies, Summer Fruit, 69
Soups
  Asparagus Soup with Lemon
    and Chives, 31
  Gazpacho, 104
Speck, Mascarpone, and
  Arugula Pizza, 146
Spinach
  Artichoke-Spinach Dip with
    Pita Chips, 49
  Egg, Ham, and Spinach Croissants, 159
  Quinoa Breakfast Bowls with Potatoes,
    Spinach, and Pesto, 64
  Vegetable Breakfast Burritos, 116
Squash
  Baked Butternut Squash Mac
    and Cheese, 193
  Vegetable Romesco Sandwiches, 105
Strawberries
  Currant Cream Scones with
    Strawberry Jam, 70
  Strawberry Cream Tartlets, 59
Sweet Chili Lime Dressing, 215
Sweet potatoes
  Roasted Winter Root Vegetables
    with Herb Butter, 192
  Sweet Potato Hash, 162

T

Tamari-Sesame Dressing, 214
Tapenade
  Black Olive Tapenade, 209
  Miyoko's Vegan Smoked Cheese
    Sandwiches, 33

Muffaletta Sandwiches, 125
Provençal Tuna Niçoise Sandwiches, 78
Roast Beef Sandwiches with Olive
  Tapenade, 126
Tarragon
  Little Gem Salad with Herbed
    Green Goddess, 54
  Rémoulade, 167
Tart Dough, 207
Tarts
  Pear-Almond Custard Tart, 199–200
  Strawberry Cream Tartlets, 59
Toasts
  Avocado Toast with Toasted Pepitas
    and Chili Crisp, 67
  Brie and Prosciutto Crostini
    with Fig Jam, 171
  Mt Tam Cheese and Bacon Jam
    Crostini, 136
  Pita Chips, 49
Tomatoes
  BLTA Sandwiches, 81
  BLT Deviled Eggs, 134
  Caprese Sandwiches with
    Balsamic Glaze, 80
  Classic Oakville Burgers, 88
  Francisco's Tomato Salsa, 209–10
  Gazpacho, 104
  Grilled Corn, Tomato, and Roasted
    Pepper Salad with Cilantro, 93
  Pesto Pasta Salad, 77
  Quinoa Salad with Tomatoes
    and Feta, 36
  Spicy Sausage, Tomato, and Fontina
    Pizza, 147
  Summer Panzanella Salad, 103
  Turkey, Bacon, and Tomato
    Sandwiches, 106
  Vegetable Wrap with Roasted
    Pepper Hummus, 50
  Watermelon, Heirloom Tomato, Feta,
    and Mint Salad, 87
Tomato juice
  Balsamic Bloody Mary, 74
  Gazpacho, 104
Tortillas
  Chorizo and Potato
    Breakfast Burritos, 115
  Vegetable Breakfast Burritos, 116
  Vegetable Wrap with Roasted Pepper
    Hummus, 50
Tuna Niçoise Sandwiches, Provençal, 78
Turkey, Bacon, and Tomato
  Sandwiches, 106

V

Vegetables. *See also specific vegetables*
  Hummus and Vegetable Crudités, 30
  Roasted Winter Root Vegetables with
    Herb Butter, 192
  Vegetable Breakfast Burritos, 116
  Vegetable Romesco Sandwiches, 105
  Vegetable Wrap with Roasted
    Pepper Hummus, 50
Vinaigrettes
  Golden Balsamic Vinaigrette, 214
  Greek Feta Vinaigrette, 214
  Lemon Vinaigrette, 213
Vodka
  Balsamic Bloody Mary, 74

W

Walnuts, Toasted, and Pear, Bitter
  Greens Salad with, 152
Watermelon, Heirloom Tomato, Feta,
  and Mint Salad, 87
Wine
  Blood Orange–Pomegranate
    Mimosa, 165
  Meyer Lemon French 69, 177
  Passion Fruit–Blood
    Orange Kiss, 139
  Peach Bellini, 84
  Summer Fruit Rosé Sangria, 57
Wraps, Vegetable, with Roasted
  Pepper Hummus, 50

Y

Yogurt
  Coconut–Chocolate Chip
    Overnight Oats, 158
  Maple-Coconut Granola and
    Yogurt Parfaits, 19
  Yogurt Panna Cotta with Fresh Figs, 151
Yountville Sandwiches, 22

Z

Zacherle, Nile, 96

Oakville Grocery | The Cookbook   223

weldonowen

PO Box 3088
San Rafael, CA 94912
www.weldonowen.com

WELDON OWEN INTERNATIONAL

CEO Raoul Goff
Publisher Roger Shaw
Associate Publisher Amy Marr
Editorial Director Katie Killebrew
VP of Creative Chrissy Kwasnik
Senior Production Manager Joshua Smith
Sr Production Manager, Subsidiary Rights Lina s Palma-Temena

Recipe Editor Kim Laidlaw
Designer Alexandra Zeigler
Photographer Erin Scott
Food Stylist Lillian Kang
Prop Stylist Glenn Jenkins

A WELDON OWEN PRODUCTION

Printed and bound in China

All rights reserved. No part of this book may be reproduced in any form without written permission from the publisher.

First printed in 2023
10 9 8 7 6 5 4 3 2 1

Library of Congress Cataloging in Publication data is available

ISBN: 979-8-88674-017-2

Oakville Grocery Co. would like to thank the many local artisans we work with every day, including Bayview Pasta, Earth & Sky Chocolates, Journeyman Meat Co., Mad Fritz Brewing Co., Model Bakery, Ohm Coffee Roasters, Point Reyes Farmstead Cheese Company, and Rancho Gordo for agreeing to be part of this beautiful book. Without you, we would not be able to provide the incredible bounty of locally grown and sustainably produced foods that make this corner of the world so unique.

Weldon Owen would like to thank Rachel Markowitz, Elizabeth Parson, and Sharon Silva.